"Wise, warm, witty, and fun. If you're tı
this is your book! Not only is *Finding Yo*
but it's also practical and down-to-eart
tactical tips. As someone who's successſ
her career multiple times, Cindy's the p̶e̶r̶s̶o̶n̶ ̶ɡ
this journey."

—Tanja Pajevic
author of *The Secret Life of Grief: A Memoir*
and *9 Steps to Heal Your Resentment and Reboot Your Marriage*

"Sharing her own pivotal experiences alongside her potent and practical process for change, Cindy Carrillo illuminates the path of possibility
and guides you back to your heart. *Finding Your Nxt*—part memoir, part
operating manual—is a compass you can return to again and again."

—Nancy Levin
author of *The Art of Change*

"As co-founders of Disruption Advisors, we have found the wisdom of
Cindy Carrillo to be indispensable, and now every business leader can have
access to her through *Finding Your Nxt*. It's jam-packed with 'what you
need to know' to make change happen in the three most important areas of
your life—your work, relationships, and lifestyle. A valuable guide!"

—Whitney Johnson, author of *Smart Growth* and *Disrupt Yourself,*
and **Amy Humble**
cofounders of Disruption Advisors

What Cindy's coaching clients say about her

"Have you ever been in a place in your life when you knew that life could be better? And you just didn't know what to do? Or even know how to create that vision or figure out what you want? 'Finding Your Nxt' allows you to open up those doors."

—**Sheila Zook**

"I was leaving a company I founded after eighteen years and had all of this experience and knowledge about my profession and running a business. And I was asking myself, 'What's next?' I can't recommend the 'Finding Your Nxt' program highly enough. For me it was a game changer—a *life* changer."

—**Jason Cormier**

"This process allowed me to home in on what are the things I really want to be spending my time, my energy, and my money on, and what to focus on to make me happy longer term as I continue to go forward and follow whatever my Nxt steps are going to be."

—**Kim O'Neil**

"I'm somebody who is always curious about professional development, and how I can enhance myself, and I also just have larger questions about what do I do Nxt and my personal Nxt as a whole, and working with Cindy gave me a chance to really reflect on what was really important to me."

—**Emily Steele**

"Talking with Cindy about 'What is my Nxt?' she's just so phenomenal at helping you work through all of these questions and potential transformation without telling you exactly what to do by opening your eyes and asking you questions, so that you can seek out things, so you can do some self-reflection and ultimately come to the answer."

—**Amy Graham**

"I went and spent some deep time with Cindy at the Ranch talking about options, where I was at, what was holding me back, trying to get all of my hang-ups out of the way, and make a decision. And I have to say that it was really a catalyst for me to move from thinking to action."

—**Trish Thomas**

"Being at the Ranch with Cindy, we were finally able to put out on the table all the things we were thinking in a safe space to understand what our options were. Some of the questions were tough and the answers even harder, but it got us to a good place and helped us take that Nxt step forward."

—**Corey Smith and Amy Humble**

"I did a lot of research on a lot of coaches and felt that Cindy really had a desire to help me. Going to her Ranch and spending time with her and Matthew was probably one of the most valuable experiences that I've had."

—**Kris Barnes**

FINDING YOUR

WHEN YOU'RE READY FOR
THE LIFE YOU REALLY WANT

CINDY CARRILLO

PUBLISHING

RIDGWAY, COLORADO

Published by
Nxt Publishing
CC Blue Enterprises LTD
244 Peaceful Way
Ridgway, CO 81432

Manuscript created in collaboration with Rick Killian,
Killian Creative, Boulder, Colorado. www.killiancreative.com

Design by Peter Gloege | LOOK Design Studio

Library of Congress Control Number: 2023912832

Paperback ISBN: 979-8-9887023-0-6
Ebook ISBN: 979-8-9887023-1-3

Printed in the United States of America
23 24 25 26 27 28 29 30 31 32 (KDP) 10 9 8 7 6 5 4 3 2 1

TABLE OF CONTENTS

next vs. Nxt

next \nekst\

(adverb): in the time, place, or order
      nearest or immediately succeeding
      I was **next** in line.

(prepostition): nearest or adjacent to
      He sat **next** to me.

(noun): the one that follows
      We're just going from one place
      to the **next**.

Nxt \nkst\ (noun)

1: the transformational phase that comes
      after your current phase of life
      (so urgent that you don't have time
      to include the "e").

2: turning a new page in your life with
      intention, to achieve fulfillment
      and purpose.

3: to find more
      It's time I found my **Nxt**.

What's Nxt?

I f you're picking up this book, I'm guessing it's because you're ready for a change—and not just a little change, but a big one. It's not that you're necessarily unhappy with your life (although that also might be the reason); it's just that you know you need to do something different, because there's *more* you could be experiencing. But you feel stuck and don't know how to figure out what specifically needs to change to tap into the kind of life you really want.

You're not alone. Change is tough—and trying to find a way to move forward on your own can be daunting and scary. But reading this book will help.

I'm always trying to get that something *more* out of life. It's not that I'm unsatisfied—I've always been *more* than satisfied with how I've lived. It's just that I invariably want (no, *need*) to look for new opportunities waiting around the corner—over and over again. I'm constantly thinking about new experiences or memories I can create, new pivots I can take, and new ideas to explore. But believe me, it's not an adventure thing (I'm not that brave or exciting), nor is it about getting more stuff (although I like nice stuff). I just believe there can always be *more*.

And I like to know what's ahead.

This has made me a bit of a control freak (some would question my use of the word *bit* here), and an Olympic-level planner (I don't go on one vacation without having the *next* vacation planned). I have a deep-seated fear that if I don't keep making up new things to do, I'll get bored. But even deeper down, I have a mad desire to keep pursuing new ways to continue to fill my life with purpose and joy.

Otherwise, what's the point?

Throughout my life, as I've moved from one phase to another (I think it's called *growing up*), I have embraced the idea of *change* in everything I do. Whether it's been about my work, my relationship(s), or my lifestyle, I've sought new ways to challenge my status quo. Because change doesn't scare me (it excites me and keeps me interested in life), I've had to learn to avoid change for change's sake, and instead make sure there's always a good reason to do something differently. To guard against my change-addiction tendencies, I've adopted the attitude, "If I'm going to take the time and expend the energy to initiate something new, it must be something *more* than I've been doing before and end up being something I *really* want to do."

Right?

Because (again) otherwise, *what's the point?*

But here's the thing: For years I didn't really have any kind of process or plan for finding the *right* change, at the right time. It was more of a "go with the flow" and "trust the powers that be" kind of change-management style—coupled with a whole lot of good fortune—that somehow worked for me in my early years but wasn't something I could count on as I grew older.

Nor was it a process I could intentionally replicate—until I started my own business.

As the founder of a company that provided work/life solutions for employees of Fortune 500 companies (which I called the Work Options Group), I discovered that the concept of change management took on a whole different level of responsibility. I had to start thinking more intentionally and strategically about how to make change happen. It wasn't *just about me* anymore, and that "go with the flow" attitude wasn't going to cut it if I wanted to grow the company. So instead of looking for opportunities just for me around each corner, I had to look for ways to expand and move the *business* forward. This is how I gained my first level of understanding about *how* to initiate and implement change successfully, not only within my organization and the people who worked for me, but with our clients as well.

Plus (if we're being honest here), it can be scary as hell to transform the life you've been living into the life you really want!

As a card-carrying member of the "change junkie" society, imagine my surprise when I discovered that change was not something most people embraced with open arms. I discovered (quickly) that most people felt uncomfortable with change, *even* if they knew a new way of doing something would ultimately make their jobs easier and more efficient. And I realized that many people believed the change process would be *painful and unnerving* and, consequently, would cause turmoil within an organization.

Crazy! I always thought change was fun!

As a newly minted CEO, this was vital information to gain *before* trying to initiate major changes within the company. I quickly realized that in order to be successful, I had to help my employees overcome their resistance and blockers to change, *then* guide them through a process of understanding the bigger *why* behind our actions. I had to define the *criteria* for them to make decisions and ultimately get them to a place of *clarity* in order to move forward. Once we did that, we were able to implement changes in a way that was *a lot less* painful and unnerving for all concerned.

As those processes continued to make themselves more self-evident, I began to learn how to distinguish between the *small changes* that needed to be accomplished within the business (the next steps) from the *bigger pivots and evolutions* that would dramatically move the company forward to the *Nxt* stages. The smaller *nexts* were the incremental day-to-day tasks needed to run the business. The larger Nxts were more transformational changes (transformations of our organization, geographic coverage, or service offerings). Both were necessary to move us forward—with the smaller *nexts* embedded in the process of achieving each Nxt—but each required a *very* different approach to change. Luckily, we became proficient at both.

It wasn't until *after* I sold my company, however, that I realized the processes we had employed for navigating both the smaller *nexts,* as well as the *Nxt-level* changes in my business, could also be applied to one's personal life (mine!).

Here I was, post-sale of the company, with the opportunity to seek significant changes in my life, and I found myself wondering, *What was Nxt?* I had no idea what I should be doing. *Me.* The woman who always jumped at making changes in her life, but now found herself *stuck* trying to figure out what was Nxt.

But then (*head slap!*) I realized I could use my business processes for change to help me navigate the Nxt-level opportunities waiting for me around the corner. Because, I realized, moving from one big change to another is a natural part of life, not just business.

Has your life taken an unexpected turn? Are you living a completely different life than you ever expected (good or bad)? Perhaps you've gotten everything out of your job and it's time to seek something new. Or your relationship with your "other" has morphed, and you need to decide whether to break it off or work on it further. Or maybe you've simply come to the end of your career, and you're wondering, *What's Nxt?*

But you're feeling stuck.

Do not despair!

Every time you make a life change, it's a chance to discover new opportunities, do something *more* than you've been doing before, and live the life you *really* want to live.

So why is it so difficult to know whether to stay the course or make a change? Because it can be confusing and overwhelming to navigate all of the options in front of you. Plus (if we're being honest here), it can be *scary as hell* to transform the life you've been living into the life you really want!

I have learned that what we really want *most* during a search for what's Nxt is *clarity*. You want to know what to expect. You want to be clear about the *what, why, where, when,* and *how* in order to see a path forward. And you want answers to all of your questions *before* you move ahead.

Which is understandable. Because change can feel painful and unnerving and scary as hell. So if you're going to invest the time and energy to initiate something new, it should be something *more* than you've been doing before, and it should be something you *really* want to do.

The first question you'll want to answer is, "Am I open to going through the *process* of transformational change?" It's not a question like, "What's for dinner tonight?" or "Where should we go on vacation this summer?" The process of finding your Nxt is a big deal. It's about starting a new and important chapter in your life. It's about wanting more—not necessarily because you are dissatisfied with your current situation, but because you know there are always more opportunities to fill your life with purpose and joy.

Everyone should be able to have more in their life, whether things are bad, mediocre, or great.

Let's face it; it's easy to initiate a change when things are bad, but what if things are actually OK or even *good enough*? Should you still be asking yourself, "What's Nxt?"

You can be *both* content with where you are and still want more—*at the same time.* You can be in a good place in your life and still *think about ways to make things even better.* Because everyone should be able to have more in their life, whether things are bad, mediocre, or great.

When I sold my business (after leading it for more than 20 years), I found myself able to do something *dramatically more.* This resulted in leaving my life as a CEO in suburbia and stepping into a whole new life as a rancher in rural Colorado. (Talk about a Nxt-level transformational change!) But let's be clear; that whole process of change was far from smooth and uneventful. There were plenty of mistakes, lessons learned, and ridiculous and awesome experiences along the way. But sitting where I am now, I can honestly say that it was *totally* worth every bit of the time and energy it took to get to this life I really wanted to live.

BOOM!

I know the process of finding your Nxt is not the same for everyone, and I'm not suggesting that everyone totally transform themselves the way I have. But there are several concepts and actionable *next* steps that I have distilled and defined based on my experiences (and outlined in this book) that I believe can be applied to *you* if you're trying to answer the question: "What's Nxt for me?"

That's why I wrote this book: to help you figure out how to successfully find and move through any type of Nxt you want to initiate—without making it painful or unnerving (it can be fun!), through the stories and lessons I've learned as I found my biggest Nxt yet.

So, let me ask you: Are you ready to *find your Nxt?*

1

Initiate a Change

CHAPTER 1

Initiate a Change

Without change there is no innovation,
creativity, or incentive for improvement.

—WILLIAM POLLARD
English Quaker writer

For more than twenty years, I had built and run my company and loved every single thing about it. And I mean every single thing, from designing our services, to scaling the business, to learning how to become a pretty damn good leader. In fact, the best part of it all was (by far) working with so many amazing people over the years.* All of the interactions, the conversations, and the knowledge and creativity they brought to the whole business process filled my soul and made me feel like I was building an extension of my family, rather than *just* a business.

---

*Shout-out to everyone who worked with me over the years!

Working in a company that I created activated every part of my being. My brain was pushed in every direction, sometimes to its limit. My heart was filled with purpose and joy every day, although there were some shitty days too. And because the company was my very own playground for instigating Nxt-level changes, I was rarely bored.

The journey to find your Nxt begins when you decide to initiate a change and step through the next door in your life.

But as tends to happen in the evolution of our lives, major shifts began to take place, which, fortunately enough, allowed me to enter the Nxt levels of my life.

On the personal side, my relationship with my husband (of twenty-three years), Brian, changed to its Nxt iteration of our relationship because we were no longer the same people we were when we got married and were raising our kids (which, by the way, I think we did exceptionally well together). Unfortunately, we were no longer able to be the people each of us wanted (or needed) the other to be.

So, instead of settling for something that wasn't quite good enough, *we* decided to redefine our relationship and make it into something that would serve us better.

And it worked. It took a bit of adjustment on everyone's part (including our kids)—and I'd be lying if I didn't admit that we all struggled with it at times—but the result after more than twenty years (post-separation) is that we are super happy with the transformation we made, and pretty damn proud of ourselves for being able to find such a wonderful Nxt level of our relationship. (Yay us!)

The result: We moved from being a wonderfully married *couple* into being a wonderfully divorced *un-couple*. And, as I'm sure you're wondering what *that* means, I'd have to say we are now two people who continue to be incredibly close; who love each other deeply and always support each other; and who not only work together to keep our family intact, but intentionally act in ways to help it thrive. And we do it all while no longer being married.

Then, about four years later, the second major shift in my life happened—this time, with my business.

Work Options Group was doing great! Our sales were up. We were winning huge contracts against our competitors (which made us as annoying as hell to them), and we were exceeding our revenue goals. We had spent the previous two years dialing in our operating, sales, and account management systems, and we had successfully launched an innovative software platform that transformed our business model. And we had a great team running the show. We were kicking ass on all fronts!

None of that was the issue.

The issue was that *my vision* for growing the company into the future was starting to dim.

It's not that I didn't enjoy the work I was doing. I still loved everything about it. But I was beginning to realize I had reached the height of my abilities to scale the company. I could no longer *see the path forward*. I could *imagine* it growing far bigger and more successful in the future. I could see that as clear as day. I just couldn't visualize how to do it with me at the helm.

My inability to see *how* to move the business forward into its Nxt stage of development was a clear signal—to me, at least—that

I was no longer the right person to be in charge. I had started it, created the vision for it, built the culture around it, and hired the right people to make it succeed. The company had reached a point where it was no longer about "making shit up" and instead was all about selling a lot more of what we had already created (which was exactly what we were shooting for). But I was always more of a "making shit up" kind of gal rather than a "sell more of what we already have" CEO. And I knew it.

Which, as it turns out, makes me a classic entrepreneur (those who like to make shit up, among other "initiate change" kinds of traits), even though I never thought of myself as one. I'm not even sure I knew what the word *entrepreneur* meant when I started my business. I just knew I had an idea about a problem I wanted to solve, and when I couldn't find any businesses out there trying to solve it, I decided to start my own company to address it.

As entrepreneurs (and a founder in my case), we typically set out to build companies with the intention of

1. providing ourselves an opportunity to design our own job, because we don't want to go out and get a real job or work for somebody else, and/or

2. if we're strategic, we begin with the intention of creating a successful business that will provide us an exit ($$) large enough to set us up for our Nxt opportunity.

My intention for the business, from the beginning, was a mix of both—to build a business I could work at over a period of time so I wouldn't have to go out and get a *real* job, and to have it lead to an eventual exit that would provide me the resources to do whatever I wanted to do moving forward.

In early 2008, I felt like I had accomplished both. Not only had I designed a great job for myself (over the course of twenty years), but the company was in a great place competitively, organizationally, *and* financially. And, as the founder, I knew I was ready to move on. As far as I was concerned, all signs pointed to the fact that it was the absolute right time to initiate an exit and sell the company. I decided to do just that.

My first step was to tell my board of directors.

Initially, they thought I was crazy. My board was composed of three gentlemen from a larger group of twenty-nine individual investors (who were *all* men, by the way), brought in a couple of years earlier during a capital raise to expand the company. Each had come in with an expectation for a healthy return on their investment within a reasonable three-to-five-year timeline. Now, just two years in, I was telling them *this* was the time to get that return.

I laid out all the factors, making the case for selling at this time, but they quickly shut me down. In their minds, we were on an upward trajectory. We should stay the course for as long as possible. And nothing I told them seemed to change their minds.

But I was still convinced this was the right time to sell.

After their initial pushback, I decided to bring in another of my (big gun) investors—who also happened to be our investment banker—and whose advice and wisdom I greatly respected. Mike listened to my rationale, asked pertinent questions, and not only agreed with my position but also agreed to make another pitch to sell the company (with me) to the board.

Mike was incredibly well-regarded by all of the board members, so they listened to his presentation intently. When they asked him why *he* was so certain *now* was the right time to sell, he said, "Over the course of my twenty-plus years of being an investment banker, I will tell you that every time a founder has said they were convinced it was the right time to sell—"

He paused and looked at me. "Cindy, are you convinced?"

I replied, "In every cell of my body."

He looked back at them and said, "They were always right."

With that, and a bit more convincing, everyone finally agreed it was the right time to sell.[*]

On September 6, 2008 (Labor Day), we put the company up for sale. Nine days later, Lehman Brothers filed for bankruptcy, the banking industry entered a long phase of turmoil, and the economy went upside down.

Now let's be clear—I did *not* see that coming, nor did I see the rest of the free fall that was about to happen. But knowing what I know now, we almost certainly would have had a hell of a time weathering the economic storm in the coming years if we hadn't sold at that time.

Remarkably, over the next couple of months (even in the midst of those crazy economic times), we went through a competitive bid process with five interested companies. This was one of the most exhilarating times of my life. I got to tell the story of our business

---

[*]OK, let's pause for a moment here. I'd be kidding you if I didn't admit that it irked me to no end that the guys on my board wouldn't accept my assessment without hearing from one of the other guys before agreeing to the sale. Even though I respected the hell out of Mike and felt a lot better getting his buy-in and support with the board, as the founder and CEO, my assessment should have been given a lot more weight initially. Unfortunately, they needed Mike to make the pitch, but fortunately for all of us they believed him. At the end of the day, none of that mattered. What mattered was that we moved forward with the sale because it was the right thing to do at the right time—for the company, for the investors, and for me.

alongside some of the smartest people I've ever had the pleasure of working with. I marveled at how these ginormous companies (*so much bigger than we were*) considered this little company I had started all those years ago to be a strong and valuable business that they now wanted to acquire it. I was bursting with pride.

At the end of a months-long process, we finalized a deal with our top competitor (who by the way, was my preferred buyer), and in late December, when the economy was imploding around us, we signed the final paperwork to sell the company. We ended up having a three-month period written into the deal that required me to get our top nine clients to approve transfers of their contracts to our acquiring company (which, amazingly, I was able to do). I stayed on for several more months to help as much as I could with the integration process. But I wasn't really needed. I was the old guard, and I was just getting in the way.

It was time for me to leave.

For real this time.

I ended up negotiating myself *out* of my contract, threw myself one hell of a "retirement" party, and, without any hesitation, turned my head toward the future. I had no idea what I was going to do, but I had an inkling it was time to create something *dramatically* different from the life I had been living. And I was definitely ready to begin the process of finding my *Nxt*.

You Get to Decide When to Initiate a Change

When was the last time you had a sense that something important needed to change in your life, and then you hit a point where you made up your mind and decided to do it? If you stop and think about it, I bet every important change you've ever made began when *you chose to initiate it.*[*] It's like facing a closed door in front of you and deciding it's the right time to open it. It's the way change begins. And I've seen it happen that way time and again.

I had a friend named Bob, whom I met shortly after moving to Colorado. He called me after finishing work on a Friday afternoon and told me that when he was driving home that day, he concluded that he hated his job. Bob had known for a while that he didn't really like the work he was doing (he talked about it often), but on this day, he admitted to himself that he truly *hated* it. Apparently, as he arrived at home and was sitting in his driveway, Bob *decided* it was time to *not only* leave his job, but also to find another career path entirely. Three months later, he went back to grad school and was off and running toward a brand-new career.

I also had a neighbor (Anna) who lived in an apartment across the hall from me when I was in college, whom I absolutely adored. She was always so cheerful and easygoing and an absolute delight to be around—until she allowed her boyfriend to move in with her. Turns out he hadn't said a decent thing to her in the

---

[*] I realize changes can happen in life due to factors beyond your control (health issues, economic downturns, and other bad stuff), and those situations might force you into finding a Nxt you would not have initiated on your own or sidetrack you from finding the Nxt you would like to pursue. For the purposes of this book, however, I will not be dealing with those situations (because it's a whole other thing), and instead will be focusing on those wonderful times in life when you have the ability to choose, and you can decide to initiate a change to live the life you really want to live.

six weeks since he moved in, and she was incredibly miserable having him there. But she felt a bit stuck and wasn't sure how to get him out.

After he said something particularly rude to her one morning, Anna *made up her mind* that she had put up with enough. She told him she was ending their relationship and he had a week to find a new place to live. The following week, Anna had her apartment to herself again and was back to being her happy self.

And then there was Tracy, who worked with me at a U.S. Senator's office in Denver. She always talked about quitting her job and moving to Italy to take cooking classes, learn about growing wine grapes, and travel throughout the country to immerse herself in the language and the culture of the country. One day, Tracy walked into the office, handed our boss her resignation, hugged me, and said, "I've decided it's time to follow my dream. Visit me in Italy!" She walked out the door. I still think of her today and smile.

Each one of these people saw a closed door in front of them and decided to initiate a change and open it. Finding your Nxt doesn't occur out of the blue; nor does it happen without your conscious intent to begin the process. The journey to find your Nxt begins when *you* decide to initiate a change and step through the next door in your life.

The Three Areas of Change

Initiating a change is not your actual Nxt—it's the first step toward finding your Nxt. To find your Nxt, you must first decide to *initiate* a change from what you are currently doing, to something else in one, two, or all three areas of your life, including:

- ✧ Your work
- ✧ Your major relationship
- ✧ Your lifestyle

In Bob's case, he initiated a change in his work when he realized he hated his job. (Yay Bob!) Once he decided to make a change, he was able to begin figuring out what was Nxt—which turned out to be entering a grad school program that took him toward a whole new career path.

Anna's change stemmed from the relationship she had with that bum of a boyfriend. Obviously, it wasn't serving her (because nobody should be that miserable in their relationship), and once she recognized that, Anna knew she had to choose whether to continue to stay the course or to change. Luckily, she ended up deciding to take her life back—and kicked her boyfriend to the curb. From that point, she was able to take some time and figure out her Nxt. (Yay Anna!)

Don't be afraid to admit when you've gone as far as you can in a job. It's much better to kick yourself out the door than to have someone else do the kicking.

Then there was Tracy. Nothing was wrong with Tracy's life when she initiated a big change. She simply wanted a much more exciting lifestyle. (Yay Tracy!) So she initiated a change in her current lifestyle to free herself up to step into the Nxt chapter of her life—in Italy. (Which still inspires me to this day.)

And finally, there were even *more* changes in the area of my relationships. I began dating a man named Matthew after Brian and I transformed our relationship. Things were going pretty well between us by the time I sold the company, so you'll start to see his name popping up in my stories from this point forward (with a lot more about us in Chapter 8—so don't stop reading!).

And so, with all of the changes in my relationships (the successful un-coupling of my marriage and becoming a new couple with Matthew), and my work (kicking myself out of a job and selling my company), and where I lived (stay tuned), I was in the process of *dramatically* changing my *entire* lifestyle.

This brings me to the next lesson of finding your Nxt: Be conscious of the ripple effects any one change can cause in the other areas of your life.

The Ripple Effects of Change

Initiating a change in your work, your relationship, or your lifestyle can initiate change *in that area of your life*, but rarely do these types of changes occur in complete isolation from the others (i.e., the change in my relationship + the change in my work = a drastic change in my lifestyle). Regardless if it's a small next step or one that requires a bigger Nxt change, it's important to think about how the ripple effects of a change in one area of your life may affect the totality of your life.

Or, in my case, how it affected a lot of other people's lives.

When I recognized I was no longer the right person to take my company forward, the decision to initiate a change in the work area of *my* life prompted a transformational change in the work area of all of my employees' lives (new owners, new leadership, new ways of doing things). In other words, the change I initiated ended up being a huge deal for a whole lot of people—*not just for me*. I really needed to think through the ripple effect and *prepare for the impact it would have on others.*

We were a pretty tight company, and I knew that most of my employees were going to be shocked, confused, and sad that I was selling the company. Change can be hard enough when you initiate it on your own, but when it's thrust upon you, it can be painful, unnerving, and scary as hell.

I also knew the news of the sale was going to prompt a rousing chorus of concern from everyone. People would be asking, "What does this mean for me?" This was a perfectly valid question, along with a ton of other questions I'd need to be prepared to answer. They'd want to know *who* was buying the company? *When* was it going to happen? *How* was it going to happen? *What* was going to change, and probably most importantly, would they still have a job?

They'd also want to know *why*? *Why* was I selling? *Why* didn't I want to run and lead the company anymore? *Why* was I changing everything?

Change is scary, and the Fear of the Unknown is powerful. Questions need answers. People need time to adjust. Understanding that when you initiate a change in your life there will most likely be a ripple effect on others in your life will help you think through and prepare how to explain the *who, what, where, when, how,* and especially the *why* behind the change you're making, providing context and answers to all those affected.

Provide Context for Changes You Initiate

We know that changes don't happen in a vacuum. And we know that change is uncomfortable for most people. So it's incredibly important to anticipate the discomfort and be prepared to provide context to those you know will be affected.

When I announced the sale of the company to my employees, it would have been irresponsible to do so without being prepared to explain the context around the change and provide as many answers as I could. So we prepared a presentation that explained the rationale, the players involved, the benefits for the company (and, hopefully, for the employees), and the reason(s) why I decided to make that change, not just for the company, but for me as well. Because they wanted (no, *needed*) to know. And even though everyone was still shocked, confused, and sad, they were given the information (with more to follow over the coming weeks) to help them navigate the change as best as possible.

> *Change can be hard enough when you initiate it on your own, but when it's thrust upon you, it can be painful, unnerving, and scary as hell.*

It's important to remember that when you go through the process of deciding to initiate a change, you live in your head for a while. You spend a lot of time thinking it all through. You think about the pros and cons, the potential risks and benefits, and the different scenarios that could play out. And once you decide, you know how and why you got there. So it's easy to forget that others haven't gone through that process with you and won't automatically understand why you decided to initiate a change. So, you need to provide them the context and help make *your* change less painful and uncomfortable *for them.*

Important Takeaways

⬥ Nxt changes happen when you decide to initiate them.

⬥ Each Nxt is typically *initiated* by a change in one, two, or all three areas in your life:

  » Your work
  » Your major relationship
  » Your lifestyle

⬥ A change in one area of your life usually creates a ripple effect into the others.

⬥ Be conscious of how a change in your life affects others, and be prepared to provide them the context they need to understand it.

⬥ When you are contemplating a change, you spend a lot of time in your head thinking it through. Remember that others aren't in your head with you and don't know your rationale for initiating a change. Bring them up to speed with what you are thinking.

⬥ Don't be afraid to admit when you've gone as far as you can in a job. It's much better to kick yourself out the door than to have someone else do the kicking.

2

Follow Your Dreams

CHAPTER 2

Follow Your Dreams

*Our imagination is the only limit
to what we can hope to have in the future.*

—CHARLES F. KETTERING
American inventor

I n the months leading up to the final closing on the sale of my company, I didn't have any idea what I was going to do, so I'd just tell people I was going to "retire." At 53, I was far too young (in my opinion) to *be* retired, but since I had no intention of starting another company or getting a *real* job, it became an easy response.

But I knew I wasn't going to *actually* retire the way most people think about it.

I wasn't going to spend my days playing golf (because I suck at it), nor was I going to "downsize" and move to a gated retirement community somewhere in Florida, with built-in activities like tennis or mahjong (not that there's anything wrong with that).

I'd even put air quotes around the word "retired" as I spoke it out loud, to make sure everyone knew that for me being retired didn't mean I was *done* working; it meant I was retiring from the way I *had been* working. Let's face it; I was still too young and too restless to retire in any traditional sense.

As the reality of the sale was beginning to sink in, however, and people really wanted to know what my future plans were (I'm not sure why it was so important to everybody else), I began embellishing my thoughts about what was Nxt. When asked about my plans, I would close my eyes and say (with a bit of dramatic flair), "I think I want to find a beautiful piece of land in the mountains where I can spend my remaining days looking out at a gorgeous view of snow-packed peaks (my hand sweeping across the sky) while sitting in a comfortable rocking chair on a covered deck, wearing a really big hat."

Obviously, it was a joke.

Because everyone knew I wasn't the *retire-in-the-mountains kind of gal.*

But people kept asking, and I kept repeating it. Mountains. Views. Deck. Big Hat? (Still not sure why the hat continued to be included.)

At first, I had no idea where that whole scenario came from, but it seemed to flow out of my mouth with ease. And then I slowly started to remember—it had been an early dream of mine when I first moved to Colorado.

When I was 19 I moved to Colorado, and before I did much else, I went on a road trip with my best friend, Nancy, to explore this great state and get the lay of the land. We had no itinerary when we hit the road and no preconceived notions about what we'd find. We allowed ourselves time to meander around, excitedly exploring this new place I was going to call home. On the third day of traveling, we stumbled upon a tiny town nestled in the San Juan Mountains (dubbed the Switzerland of America), and I instantly fell in love with the whole area. As we drove from one spot to another, I thought my heart was going to explode from the beauty of the mountains looming everywhere. I remember declaring *very loudly* in the car, "I have no idea when or how I'm gonna do it, but someday I'm gonna live close to these mountains and look at these views every single day of my life."

I dreamt about living in those mountains for months following that road trip, but as *real life* took over, it faded into one of those idealistic dreams that got stored on a dusty old shelf in the back of my brain, where it stayed for more than thirty-five years.

Until the day after the deal was signed and the company was no longer mine.

With the company sold and my kids well into their own lives, I had no real responsibilities tying me to any particular place. I found myself at a pivotal point in life. I had initiated this huge change and now had the opportunity and the funds to come up with a big Nxt dream for myself, which was potentially bigger than I'd ever dreamt before.

So I started to pay closer attention to the *idea* behind the words I jokingly spoke of in my retirement fantasy. I changed my perspective about finding a beautiful piece of land in the mountains, with gorgeous views—from being a joke to asking myself "Why not?"

Why shouldn't I find a piece of land in a beautiful location with gorgeous mountain views? I had the time, desire, and resources.

So why shouldn't it be my Nxt?

No reason. No reason at all.

So I *decided* to make it so.

Just the thought of exploring the area that Nancy and I visited all those years ago, this time with the very real possibility of finding a beautiful piece of property overlooking *those* mountains, brought a level of excitement I hadn't experienced in years.

It felt like the perfect opportunity to create something new for myself, something different from anything I had done before. I had no real idea what that meant, or what parts of my life would be impacted by it, but if there was a dream to make true in all of this, this seemed to be the time and place to begin figuring out if this was where my Nxt could be.

So I picked up the phone and called a local Realtor to begin the search to make my dream come true.

You Get More Than One Dream

How many times have you been told you should have *one* purpose in life, which will give you meaning, as if all of life were meant to be one accomplishment? Or you should find *one* big passion to work on your entire life? Or *one* big audacious lifelong dream to work toward?

Your *whole* life?

And, if that's not enough, how many times have you heard that once you achieve that one big audacious dream, you can *finally* relax, begin to enjoy your life, and be happy? As if the time you spent living your life along the way was just for the purpose of getting to that one big dream at the end of the rainbow.

But what do you do after that?

What if, instead of trying to create one big dream to drive you forward, you allow yourself to have *a bunch* of dreams *along the way*? One dream at one stage of your life, followed by the Nxt dream, and the Nxt, and the Nxt, and so on. Little dreams that take you from one place in your life to the Nxt. Why should you put all of your eggs into one dream basket when, instead, you could benefit from having a bunch of dreams, allowing you to learn as you go and evolve from one dream to the Nxt?

What if, instead of trying to create one big dream to drive you forward, you allow yourself to have a bunch of dreams along the way?

Nxt dreams are the visions you see for each step in the journey of your life. They're ideas you believe are important enough to explore. Reflections of the life you aspire to have *Nxt*. Not at the end of your life, but just around the corner. They shouldn't be so big and so out of reach that you can never hope to attain them. But at the very least, they should be something *more*, or different, than what you are doing now.

So what if you've had only one big audacious dream you've been working toward and you've spent your entire life totally focused on getting there? Am I telling you to stop it and find a new dream? Absolutely not! Keep going if you believe that one dream is going to be the rock-star dream of your lifetime! *But* you don't have to wait for that one dream to come true to find enjoyment or become happy in another. It doesn't have to be your one measure of success and fulfillment in life. You can build smaller dreams on top of it— and all around it—essentially living a bunch of smaller dreams along the way until you get to the big-bang finish of your big audacious dream.

> The universe is a vast and magical place, but it does not make your dreams come true. You do.

I know dreaming can feel a bit daunting. And it's easy to believe you get only a finite number of dreams in your lifetime. I found myself feeling like I was tapped out in the dream department after I sold the company. Faced with such a major opportunity for change in my life, the only thing I could describe myself doing was "retiring," even though I knew I wasn't done.

But it was the message I kept receiving over and over again.

"You did great. You built a company and sold it. Now you can finally relax and begin to enjoy your life and be happy." But I *had been* enjoying my life all along. I was exceedingly happy. I didn't think I was close to being done. Yet, when the dream of finding a beautiful piece of property in the mountains kept presenting itself—albeit in the form of a joke at first—I had to give myself *permission* to have yet another dream, and ask myself, "Why shouldn't it be my Nxt dream?"

The difference between what you might have been taught about having one big audacious dream your *whole life* and the process of finding your Nxt is that each stage of your life *can* have its own dream, and its own Nxt. As life evolves—and you gain new information, new experiences, and a lot more knowledge about yourself and the world you live in—you get to create your Nxt dream over and over and over again. Big dreams, small dreams—it doesn't matter. You can continue to dream and make Nxts, again and again.

How to Know Which Dream to Follow?

Once you get the hang of dreaming, you might find that you start dreaming all the time. It can be addicting when you realize there are tons of possibilities to pursue. But not all dreams are worth exploring. It's best to be picky and develop a level of rigor when deciding which Nxt dream you want to spend your time and energy moving toward.

Your Nxt dream should *not* be a frivolous idea that you throw out *into the universe* without any intention of participating in attaining it. The universe is a vast and magical place, but it does not make your dreams come true. *You do.*

Secondly, Nxt dreams must have some basis in reality, considering your skills, strengths, attitude, and desires. Seriously, don't make your Nxt dream a fantasy composed of unrealistic things with no relationship to who you are or how you want to live. You may dream about becoming a neurosurgeon, but if you suck at science and math and have a deep aversion to blood, that would be an utterly foolish dream for you to spend your valuable time and energy pursuing. So dreaming about becoming a neurosurgeon would be a fantasy, not your Nxt.

Ideally, your Nxt dream will be an idea that inspires you to ask and answer a ton of questions—and gets your heart palpitating with excitement. You'll feel like you can almost reach out and touch it. It might be something you began thinking about years ago but weren't *quite* ready to reach for (like my dream of living in the mountains with a gorgeous view). Or it could be something you recognize as the natural next step you should take to get you where you want to go. It doesn't matter *when* your dream began; it matters that you recognize *it is worthy of your time and energy* to make that dream come true.

Capitalize On What You Do Best

Another important component for choosing your Nxt dream is to capitalize on things you do best and thrive while doing them. You might be a great salesperson or product developer or team leader. Or you might be an amazing designer or artist. Whatever it is, I'm sure there are many things in your skill set that you can pull from. The key is to identify which things you do well *and* thrive doing and stop focusing on who you are not but wish you could be. (As in my wish to become a tall, willowy model who can make an astounding crème brulé while being the CEO of her own Fortune 100 company—especially if you're only five foot three.) Capitalize instead on what you do best and what you love doing.

Everyone has things they're really good at, but as simple humans, we tend to take them for granted because we think, if *we* know how to do them, it's probably no big deal. We figure, "Because I know how to do x, y, or z, everyone else must know how to do x, y, or z as well." We assume everyone else in the room knows what we know, because we don't think we're special.

But I'm here to tell you: *You are special.* Not everyone can do what you do, and not everyone knows what you know. So it's time you came to terms with the fact that you have superpowers. Identify them, embrace them, and use them to make your Nxt dream come true.

Important Takeaways

- You get to enjoy more than one big audacious dream in your life. In fact, you get to have a whole bunch of dreams in your life.

- Each stage of your life gets its own dream— and its own Nxt.

- Nxt dreams must have some basis in reality, considering your skills, strengths, attitude, and desires.

- Don't pursue a fantasy dream. It's not worth your time and energy.

- You have superpowers: Identify them, embrace them, and use them.

- If you ever take a road trip with your best friend and discover a place that takes your breath away, *try to remember it*. It might end up being the place to make a dream come true.

3

Break the Blockers

CHAPTER 3

Break the Blockers

Anything you say before
the word "but" doesn't count.

—KEVIN KELLY
Senior Maverick and co-founder, *Wired* magazine

*I*n the spring of 2009, I called a Realtor I knew in southwestern Colorado and told her about the (silly) dream I had about "retiring" on a beautiful piece of land with a gorgeous view, and how I thought I was ready to start looking at properties in the area. I also told her I was unsure about any other details to help narrow down the search.

Michelle was more than happy to help. She was a wealth of information about the area, the types of properties on the market, and the local culture. (Ranching culture is *very* different from suburban culture.) *But* before exploring properties, she wanted to help me narrow down what I hoped to find.

In other words, she needed more information than "I'm looking for a beautiful piece of land with a gorgeous view."

She began with a list of questions. (SPOILER ALERT: Her questions weren't crazy, off-the-wall Realtor questions. They were questions you would expect *anyone* to be able to answer if they were searching for property in *any* location.)

They were questions like:

- ✧ "What size property are you thinking about?"

- ✧ "Are you looking to build from scratch, or are you wanting a house that is move-in ready—or maybe requires some remodeling to meet your needs?"

- ✧ "Do you want to live *in* the mountains or have a *view* of the mountains?"

- ✧ "What are you planning to do with the land?"

- ✧ "Do you want to have neighbors nearby or live in a more remote area?"

- ✧ "Will this be a full-time home or a second home?"

- ✧ "Is this home a short-term investment, or is this something you see yourself stepping into as a big part of your future?"

Wow!

I didn't know the answers to *any* of these questions and responded with something like, "Hmmmm. I don't think I've really thought about that"—which was utterly embarrassing.

It also made me realize this Nxt dream thing wasn't a joke. Nor was it a frivolous pursuit. It was a big deal. It was about the Nxt stage of my life, and I needed to think *deeply* about what I wanted that to look like.

I had spent the past twenty-or-so years being married to Brian, raising my two wonderful kids, and building a great business in Boulder County. I volunteered. I had a solid group of friends, was a part of the community, and felt like I had put down deep roots over the years. I knew *that* life, and it was comfortable. But I also knew I had an opportunity to design something different for my life. Which meant stepping into something new. Something unknown. And, potentially, something I wasn't certain I'd be able to do.

In April, Matthew and I met Michelle in Ridgway and began our search. We chose to look at properties with existing houses on them and toured about a dozen different listings in various configurations. Some with lots of acreage, some smaller, some with newer houses, and some with older, needs-some-work houses.

With every listing, I'd see the possibilities, *but* I also focused on the faults. I'd say things like, "This house is the perfect size for us and the kitchen is nice, *but* I can't imagine how we'd make it work if the kids or our friends came for a visit." Or, "What a great setup on the property, *but* those huge trees are blocking the view."

Each place offered possibilities, *but* nothing seemed to have it all.

After two days of touring properties (and round after round of "this is great, *but . . .*"), we went for coffee with Michelle to review what we had seen and talk about next steps. All I could talk about were each property's faults. This wasn't like me. I've always been a *half-full* kinda gal. I was feeling dejected, and it was becoming clear that something more was going on with me.

In a conversation with Matthew before heading home, it all came out as "I know it would be really cool to have some land in this area, *but* it's a six-hour drive from Boulder. And *what if* our family and friends won't visit us? And what do we know about ranching—*what if* we can't figure out how to make it work?"

Clearly, I was blocked and shutting down everything about this dream before we even got started. All I could see were the *"buts"* and the *"what ifs,"* and they were keeping me from moving forward and from seeing the things I wanted (and needed) in order to move forward.

If I was going to find my Nxt, I needed to stop focusing on all the things that *could* stop me from moving ahead and start looking for ways to make my dream come true. Finding your Nxt begins with a willingness to change your perspective from what you *think you know* to what *could be.*

Three Blockers of Change

How many times have you stopped yourself from moving into your Nxt because you have no idea what the future looks like, and that Fear of the Unknown is worse than staying where you are? Or how about those times you worried that if you did step forward, you might fail? Or maybe you believe it's easier to settle for what you have rather than exert the time and effort to try to make things better?

There are many reasons you can be blocked from moving into your Nxt, but I've found you can sum them up as the *Three Blockers of Change*:

- ✧ Fear of the Unknown
- ✧ Fear of Failure
- ✧ Willingness to Settle

Each Blocker of Change is like a big red stop sign set up to keep you from seeing *what could be*. Each is designed to stop you dead in your tracks *before* you begin to consider what's Nxt. And because each is so insidious, you can experience one blocker at a time or multiple blockers at the same time, making it difficult to pinpoint which one is really blocking you from moving forward.

When you're blocked, it can feel like an insurmountable barrier. But experiencing any one of these blockers is not an indication that you're *uninterested* in finding your Nxt. It's common to *want* to change and yet find yourself paralyzed from taking the next step, *because* you're experiencing one or more of these blockers.

I certainly found it challenging to break through my blockers to open myself up to the possibilities. Understanding that I was blocked, however, allowed me to change my perspective of how I was approaching change and get out of my own way to get my Nxt dream going.

Fear of the Unknown

During the early stages of finding your Nxt, nothing is tangible and it can feel scary as hell. You might have snippets of an idea or dream, but it looks and feels more like a piece of Swiss cheese—with really big holes—than a solid, smooth dream laid out in front of you. And because your mind and imagination like things to be solid and smooth, they often fill in the blanks with scary possibilities (instead of rainbows and puppies), creating all kinds of dark visions in the void of the unknown.

Each Blocker of Change is like a big red stop sign set up to keep you from seeing what could be.

The Fear of the Unknown has ways of sneaking around to give you the illusion of wanting to figure out what's Nxt, while keeping you from moving forward by using the word *but* in a sentence to discount an idea or possibility.

Let me explain how it shows up.

You begin with a positive statement—followed by a *"but"*—which is then followed by another statement that essentially negates the positive statement.

It goes like this: "I would absolutely love to move to the mountains, *but* I'm sure I won't be able to find a piece of land in the perfect location."

It starts with a positive statement, "I would absolutely love to move to the mountains"—which *appears* like you're open to the possibilities—followed by a *"but"* and then the second statement: "I'm sure I won't be able to find a piece of land that is in the perfect location." This totally *negates* the first part of the sentence.

In one fell swoop, you've blocked any movement forward, based on what you *assume* to be true—which is based on a fear of exploring the unknown. Most of us don't recognize this as a mechanism for blocking ideas at the start of the exploration process. It's an effective blocker that shuts you down early, keeps you from gathering important information to fill in the blanks, and keeps the unknown void looking daunting.

Fear of Failure

Even the possibility of failure can be enough to block you from exploring opportunities and possibilities that could enhance your life. This fear, like the Fear of the Unknown, can stop you from gathering information early on and undermine your ability to determine whether the risk of failure really exists—or not.

But that's not even the real problem.

The real problem is that the standard definition for *failure* is a "lack of success" or the "inability to perform a normal function."[*] So when you apply that to the idea of doing something you have never done before, well then, of course you'd have a total fear of doing that!

But here's the real truth: Failure occurs *only* when there is *no learning* achieved from the experience. Let me repeat

---

[*]"Failure," Merriam-Webster.com, 2023. https://www.merriam-webster.com (accessed July 17, 2023).

that—failure occurs *only* when there is *no learning* achieved from the experience.

If you engage in something with good intentions and make a good-faith effort to accomplish something, and it doesn't work, OK.

Ask yourself, "What have I learned?"

"How can I do better the next time?"

"What mistakes would I avoid?"

"How would I move forward differently?"

If you can answer these questions and learn from a mistake or a misstep, you have not failed. Period.

The Fear of Failure also reveals itself in the *what if* questions that emerge when you are looking for your Nxt.

"*What if* our family and friends won't visit us if we move six hours away?"

"*What if* we can't figure out how to be ranchers?"

"*What if* we end up disliking rural life?"

All of these questions were based on what I was afraid would *not* work, *before* seeking the answers that would help to make them work. I was simply afraid of failing.

The Fear of Failure also brings out all kinds of emotions tied to the *perceived* consequences of not doing well at what you set out to do.

Perceived fear: "What will my family think?"

Consequence: If I fail, they'll be disappointed in me and think I'm a rotten mom/daughter/sister/ex-wife/cousin/aunt/etc.

Perceived fear: "What if I put my time and money into making a change and it turns out to be the wrong choice?"

Consequence: If I fail, everyone will think I'm a dumbass fool for wasting a bunch of time and money on this crazy idea.

When we don't know how to predict a successful outcome, we give in to the Fear of Failure as a reason to stop us from moving ahead. We make up a bunch of perceived consequences so we can block ourselves from ever uncovering the possibility of success (even though we know no one is going to think we're a rotten family member or a dumbass fool).

When we don't know how to predict a successful outcome, we give in to the Fear of Failure as a reason to stop us from moving ahead.

The truth is, change can be time-consuming and unpredictable, and when you're looking for your Nxt, you'd like to have as much certainty about the outcome early on. But at the early stages of exploring what's Nxt, that's not always possible. Many questions must be asked. A lot of information must be gathered, and you'll go through several time-consuming iterations that may or may not provide the level of certainty you're hoping for. This means you'll need to *believe in* what you're doing and have some *patience* to work through the process (neither of which has ever been my strong suit).

But here's the thing: If you let this blocker stop you from beginning the process, you'll probably end up staying where you are, possibly settling for something less than what you want.

So take a minute. Breathe. If you chose a dream that capitalizes on your strengths, gather all the information you need to confidently decide, and set out to learn through the process. I promise you—*you won't fail*. And if you do make a mistake in the process (which is almost guaranteed, because it takes trial and error to get things right), promise yourself that you'll learn, learn, learn all along the way.

Willingness to Settle

How often do you settle for things in your life, things that might not be what you *really* want, but you tell yourself, "It's OK. It's good enough"?

It's not uncommon. We all have times when we go through the motions of doing what we're doing—Willing to Settle because we think it's easier than initiating a change. You may have forgotten the purpose behind why you started something, but you stay where you are rather than start something you haven't done before (Fear of the Unknown) or try something new that you're afraid won't work (Fear of Failure).

> *You may think it's easier to stay where you are, but it actually isn't easier to settle.*

Rather than expend the energy to give definition and dimension to something new, you hold on to what you have because you know what it is. Knowing what you have gives you a feeling of stability *even if it's not serving you anymore* (which is the trap of blocking yourself through your Willingness to Settle).

Sometimes you settle because you feel like you must take what you can get, or you don't feel like you have the time or energy to make a change. Or you've been taught that you should be grateful for what you have (even if it's not meeting your needs). You find yourself three years into a job you disdain because your supervisor is a nitpicky micromanager, the work wouldn't challenge a third grader, and the job is sucking your soul dry. But you stay because 1) at least you get a paycheck, 2) you know how to do the work, and 3) it would take a lot of time and effort to look for another job. So you settle. Even though it doesn't serve you and it makes you miserable.

Here's another truth you may not want to hear if you are currently settling for something that is not serving you (but you are sticking around because it *might* get better): You may think it's easier to stay where you are, but it actually *isn't* easier to settle. It takes a lot of rationalizing and coping to settle for something that isn't working. It's exhausting and unpleasant. And here's the kicker: It's exhausting and unpleasant for everyone around you.

Hopefully, you'll now understand and believe that settling for something that is not serving you is not worth it. It's not worth your time or your energy. And if you don't already know this—you deserve more. Lots more.

So whatever script you have going through your head that has you convinced that you shouldn't ask for more, expect more, or want more because you are not worthy—I want you to rip that sucker up and throw it away. Then I want you to dig down inside yourself and begin to dream again. Because dreaming is the #1 most-effective way to kick your Willingness to Settle in the proverbial ass.

Breaking Through the Blockers

Learning about the Blockers of Change, recognizing them, and seeing them for what they are will help you kick them out of the way so you can move toward finding your Nxt. Like it or not, you can't move into your Nxt dream or your Nxt stage in life *until* you learn how to identify and break through the blockers that are stopping you.

How did I break through my blockers so I could move on to my Nxt dream?

First, I stopped using *but*. Instead, I'd say "and . . ."
Whenever I found myself about to use the word *but*, I'd change it to the word *and*. This forced me to think about how I could address the challenge I was facing *and* not be blocked by it.

I stopped saying, "This house is the perfect size for us and the kitchen is nice, *but* I can't imagine how we'd make it work if the kids or our friends came for a visit." I changed the *"but"* to *"and,"* adding, ". . . and if we love it enough to buy it, we'd need to expand the footprint and/or build a guest house to accommodate our family and friends."

Now the decision about whether the house would work was based on whether or not we loved the place enough to make that additional investment by laying out some criteria and a solution. The decision to proceed wasn't about whether the dream was worthy or not, but whether that particular piece of property would meet the specific criteria we defined as accommodating visiting family and friends.

Using the word *and* sets you up to use a different perspective when approaching an opportunity. Instead of shutting it all down (throwing the proverbial baby out with the bathwater), it allows you to address an area of concern and explore under what circumstances you might be able to make things work.

Second, I stopped looking for problems and started looking for solutions.

Instead of focusing all of my thoughts on the Fear of the Unknown by focusing on a problem—like, "What if we move down here and have no place to accommodate our family and friends who come to visit?"—I changed my approach to the unknown by identifying a potential solution to the problem: "What if we built a guest house to accommodate our friends and family traveling to see us. Would that make it more attractive for people to visit us?"

This turned a potential problem, based on the unknown, into a potential solution.

Another example of what was blocking me was my concern, "What if we end up building this place, and we hate living in a rural area?" That's a valid concern, right?

Dreaming is the #1 most-effective way to kick your Willingness to Settle in the proverbial ass.

You don't want to move somewhere you feel out of place. Instead of letting it block me from moving forward, I changed the way I addressed that concern from thinking of it as an unknown fear, *"What if* I hate it?"—to looking for a way to solve it.

When I did that, it became: "I think it would be a good idea to spend some time in the area to see if we like it before we commit to buy property and move there." Much better. Address the unknown by getting to know the place! Now I had a way to address the problem. If we ended up not liking rural life, we would face it and strike out on a different path.

The reality is, you don't know a lot of things until you try them. You don't have all the answers *until* you ask the questions and seek the information to fill in the blanks. That's how it happens with almost everything you do in life. The *buts* and the *what ifs* aren't bad. They help identify, early on, your fears of failing and the unknown. What really stops you is when you don't recognize them and don't change your perspective to address them. Those who are brave enough to push through their blockers are able to move forward. Those who allow the blockers to stop them stay where they are.

Third, I stopped giving the Fear of Failure any power.
I recognized that if I set out on my Nxt with the intention of learning and growing from the experience, the Fear of Failure would lose all its power over me. I decided that mistakes were not just a possibility in my Nxt, but an absolute. I realized I'd have to figure things out along the way. I embraced the idea of trial and error and released myself from the fear that if I made a mistake, I would somehow be considered a failure.

I was prepared to learn from my experience, so the prospect of failure no longer existed.

Finally, I refused to settle.
I just refuse to settle. Ever. As I've said from the start of this book, I always want to live the life I really want to live. Therefore, there is absolutely no room to settle.

Period.

Important Takeaways

◇ The three Blockers of Change are

  » Fear of the Unknown,
  » Fear of Failure,
  » Willingness to Settle.

◇ The Fear of the Unknown appears when you use the word *but* in a sentence to discount an idea or possibility.

◇ Try replacing *but* with *and*—it is much more solution-oriented.

◇ The Fear of Failure most often reveals itself in *"What if . . ."* questions.

◇ Failure occurs only when there is no learning achieved from an experience. So learn and keep incrementally improving—then there is no failure.

◇ You are generally Willing to Settle because:

  » You feel like you have to take what you can get,
  » You don't feel like you have the energy or time to make a change, or
  » You've been taught that you should be grateful for what you have and that should be enough.

None of these are true.

◇ See the Blockers for what they are and kick them out of the way so you can move forward.

◇ If nobody has told you this lately: *You deserve more.*

4

See What's Nxt

CHAPTER 4

See What's Nxt

The first step toward creating an improved
future is developing the ability to envision it.

—TONY DUNGY
Pro Football Hall of Famer

*L*ater in the spring, Matthew and I drove back to Ridgway to
meet Michelle to look at more properties. This time I was
excited because I had a new framework (and I wasn't blocked anymore) about what kind of house and property I wanted. I had been
thinking about my favorite home, one I had lived in with Brian and
the kids (which held a very special place in my heart), and I made
a mental list of everything I loved about it.

It was in the mid-1980s when Ally was about two and I was
pregnant with A.J. that Brian and I found a house we fell in love
with in rural Boulder County. Brian and I bought it at a time
when we probably couldn't afford it, but it struck every chord for

that dream house we had been looking for. So we took a risk and went for it.

We called it the *Big House* (as we still fondly refer to it).

The Big House sat on five open acres in an unincorporated part of the county. It made us feel like we were living out in the country. In reality, it was more country*ish*, as we were only about ten miles away from town. Still, our neighbors were far enough away that none of us could see inside each other's windows, so I felt it met the technical definition of country*ish*.

Realizing your dream begins when you can see an ideal version of it laid out in front of you.

Living there gave us the illusion of a rural life while still being close enough to every kind of store and convenience (like a grocery and a Target) that we needed to raise our two kids and keep them entertained, but still be far enough away to keep us intentional about "running out" to pick up a few things.

We were also surrounded by open space (nature), which we loved. We'd find deer grazing on the lawn, hear coyotes howling in the distance, and spend hours relaxing on the couch, gazing out our two-story bay window, watching the weather patterns move in over the horizon. Best of all, the Big House was a great space for gathering with family and friends and creating memories.

I thought we had absolutely hit the jackpot when we moved there.

Before starting our next search, I made a list of everything I loved about the Big House and asked Michelle to see what she could find to meet any or all of the criteria:

1. A large parcel of land (maybe ten acres) to provide opportunities to do cool things.

2. A property that felt country*ish*, ensuring we'd be close enough to conveniences like grocery stores, a hardware store, restaurants, and, of course, a Target. (Hey, who doesn't want access to a Target when you need it?)

3. Close proximity to nature—which was, by definition, the area we were looking at.

4. Beautiful views—lest we not forget where this whole dream started.

5. A place special enough to make memories.

Michelle accepted the challenge and was off and running to look for properties to meet our criteria, but the real game changer turned out to be our timing. It was 2009, and the housing bubble had burst wide open. Real estate sales across the country had slowed down dramatically, and prices were being reduced everywhere, especially in rural areas. For us, this meant we were able to look at much larger pieces of property than the ten acres I originally thought would be in our price range.

On our next trip down to Ridgway, Michelle showed us a lovely 1970s-era farmhouse that checked *almost* all of our boxes. It was located on thirty-five acres in a beautiful valley below a magnificent mountain range (yes, the views were gorgeous), with a house nestled in some trees, making it feel cozy and quiet. It was close enough to conveniences but still far enough away for us to need to be intentional about how often we would go into town. It wasn't perfect, as the farmhouse needed a lot of work, but there was plenty of potential on the property for it to be my dream home.

The property itself was larger than anything I had dreamed of owning, and (way) out of our price range, but we figured it was worth a try to see if they'd come down to a more affordable number. So we made an offer. A really *low* offer (50 percent below the asking price), because the asking price was pretty high, the economy was pretty bad, and there were *no other buyers* in the area.

I figured, *Maybe we'd get lucky?*

Nope. The owners got offended and didn't take the offer seriously. They pretty much told us to jump in a lake (their actual response was a bit more graphic, but you get the idea). Surprisingly, I felt relieved. It *wasn't* perfect. A good portion of the land was not suitable for animals and farming (which I didn't even realize was such a big deal *until* they rejected the offer), and the farmhouse was pretty small. It would have required a lot of remodeling to make it into a guest house. *Plus,* we'd still need to build a main house for us to live in.

I could have made a counteroffer (or at least a more reasonable offer based on their asking price), but that would have felt like I was settling for something that was still beyond my budget and wasn't really meeting all of my criteria. So we walked away from that property and told Michelle we'd like to return in a month or so to resume the search. However, based on this experience, I thought we should probably look for something smaller because—maybe, just maybe—I had gotten a little cocky and should probably step my dream down a notch.

But then—*drumroll, please*—a week later the landowner from the property next door (about twenty acres away) called Michelle and said, "I hear there's a buyer looking for some land in the valley." Michelle said, "Yes, and they love the area, but your property's list price is *way* out of reach for their budget."

His property had been on the market for *a lot* more than the other property, so we hadn't even considered it. Plus it had *nothing* on it. No house. No electricity, no water, no gas, and no services at all. It was thirty-five acres of very expensive, undeveloped pastureland.

Then he told Michelle, "Well . . . I'd be willing to sell my property for the *same price they offered the neighboring property*—if they're interested."

Stop the music! Michelle was dumbfounded. He had just offered us an *amazing* deal!

We had to take a closer look at it.

A week later we stood on that property and looked out at the most beautiful, calming, majestic views we had ever seen. The entire San Juan Mountains were spread out across the horizon, and gorgeous green pastures led up to a small rise that we knew would be the perfect spot for a main house. Just off to the west was an ideal location for a guest house. Everything about it was so open, and the views were so magnificent. It truly took my breath away.

But this was also a much more *dramatic* Nxt level change than anything we had been thinking about (e.g., having to create a whole new life from the ground up). So we needed to stay calm, remain thoughtful, and think intentionally about moving forward with this deal.

The crazy thing was that I could *see* my dream unfolding before my eyes on that land. I couldn't see the exact house we would end up building, or where the garden would go, or the kinds of animals we'd have one day, but I could *see* the possibilities for building it all. I could see animals grazing in the pastures and food growing in the garden. I could see our family and friends hanging out with us, hear their laughter, and imagine the memories we could create there. As I stood on that property and closed my eyes, I could see the Nxt chapter of my life laid out before me.

And it filled me up.

I looked over at Matthew, who was gazing out over the property, and I knew he could see it too. I saw it in the way his eyes swept across the pastures and around the boundaries of the property. We held hands, walked the entire perimeter, and talked about the possibilities of what this land could be and how it provided the opportunity to create something totally new.

We made our way back to where Michelle was waiting for us. As the three of us looked over the property, she asked, "Can you see yourselves living here?"

I laughed (not a joking kind of laugh, but a knowing one) and said, "Ya know, we can."

What Do You *See*?

In the early stages of finding your Nxt, it's important to define what you want your Nxt *to do for you*. At this point in the process, you probably won't be able to define the specifics of how you'll do it, but you can use your mind's eye to visualize the *big picture* of how your dream can play out in your future. You'll have plenty of time to dig into the details once you've had the chance to focus on your idea, so don't force yourself to dig in too deeply too quickly. Take your time. Watch your dream unfold before your eyes and imagine the possibilities of what *could be*.

For me, as I looked out across those thirty-five acres, I could visualize making a life on that land. I could see the possibilities for building a home, tending a garden, and caring for animals. More importantly, I could see my children (and their children), as well as all our family and friends spending time on the property. If I closed my eyes, I swear I could hear their laughter in the air.

For you, it might be seeing yourself in a new career—expanding your horizon to do the kind of work you've always dreamed of. Or maybe you can see building a life with someone new—getting married (or not), raising kids (or not), and experiencing life together. You might even see yourself moving from the small town where you grew up to a city where you've always dreamed of living or, like me, the other way around.

Whatever it is, taking the first step toward realizing your dream begins when you can *see* an ideal version of it laid out in front of you. What does that new career ideally look like? What would your best life feel like if you could spend it with your true love? Or, if you could imagine the most wonderful way to live in that big city of your dreams, what kind of life would that be?

Sometimes You Have to Close
Your Eyes to See Clearly

At this stage of finding your Nxt, you have the opportunity to define the *ideal version* of what your dream could do to enhance your life. It's not about listing the specific details about how it will work. Believe me, that will come later on, when you have enough information to create a plan to move forward. Right now, just close your eyes and imagine the possibilities.

When you close your eyes, you're not limited by what you already see. You can paint a picture of the *possibilities* you want to create and design for yourself. You can use broad strokes to illustrate what you want your dream to feel like and do for you, allowing yourself to describe an ideal scenario for how you want your Nxt *to be,* with no constraints. No blockers getting in your way. No details about how you'll do it. No limitations. Just a wide-open description of the big picture of what your Nxt step would do for you.

I had a coaching client (Tim) who was really unhappy with his job. He wanted to work with me to find his Nxt career move. When I asked him to tell me what he thought he'd like to do Nxt, he gave me a list of details for the job he thought he wanted. He said he wanted to get a program design job (with a specific title), in financial services, where he could work remotely but still could be connected to a team. When I asked him *why* he wanted those specific things, he responded, "That's what I've always done in the past, so that's what I figured I should do again."

Hmmmm, I thought. *That doesn't sound much like a career move.*

When I asked him if he could describe the bigger picture of

what he hoped his new job would *do for* him, he was confused and unsure what I was asking him to do. He shifted in his chair and started talking about the salary he thought he could get, the hours he wanted to work, and the amount of vacation he wanted to get as part of his "package." More details, but nothing indicating *why* he wanted to do that kind of work.

The reality was that he couldn't imagine doing anything else.

The type of work Tim described was all that he knew and all he assumed he could do. He had never asked himself *why* he did that kind of work. He knew he was good at it, and his superiors confirmed that with pay raises, promotions, and bonuses, and since his last job had been in the financial services industry (and he did well there), he figured that was what he was best suited to do moving forward.

I asked Tim to close his eyes and imagine doing work that would *excite and challenge* him. He sat back, closed his eyes for about ten seconds, squirmed for a bit, and then opened them. He said, "I have no idea what that would look like."

Tim had forgotten how to dream. It was more comfortable for him to talk about the specifics of what *he'd done before* rather than reimagine what he *could possibly do in the future*. To get Tim to expand his vision, I suggested he try to think about the ideal ways in which he'd like to work, instead of focusing on the job he had been doing, and in doing so, base that vision on capitalizing on all of his strengths and skills, as well as what he loved to do.

I asked him to close his eyes again, take a deep breath, and tell me what *working* would look and feel like if he could design it to be everything he wanted it to be.

"*Anything* I want it to be?"

"Yes," I said. "Hell, if you're going to take the time and effort to step into something new, why not begin by imagining how you'd design it for yourself?"

Tim closed his eyes (again) and slowly began to describe the ideal way in which he would want to work. He talked about capitalizing on the areas of design he thrived on, collaborating with members of a team, working in a company that valued his input and suggestions, and exploring how he'd like to be responsible for developing new systems that would be meaningful and useful to a company. Tim realized he thrived when he was able to focus on his area of expertise, collaborate with others, make an impact within his company, and be appreciated for his work.

He opened his eyes and said, "I think I can now see *how* I want to work." *Yes!*

We kept talking, he kept seeing more, and, eventually, Tim was able to define what he wanted his Nxt *to do for him.*

If you're thinking about changing careers like Tim was, begin by letting go of the jobs you've had in the past. Instead, imagine what *working* would look like if you could design it for yourself. How would it capitalize on your strengths and skills? How would it challenge and please you? Think about *how* you'd like to work with others, *why* the work would be important to you, and in *what* ways you could grow within the job.

Be Open to the Evolution of Your Dream

Rarely is the first iteration of your dream the one you end up fully pursuing. It's amazing how many twists and turns your initial idea will take as you begin to search out the right path to finding your Nxt. As you gather more information, refine your thinking and discover more opportunities as they present themselves, you'll often come to a place where your Nxt is a different version—most often a *better* version—of the original dream you thought you wanted.

When I first began my search for property, I imagined finding a house on a lot that provided a beautiful view of the mountains. That was it. So that's where we began our search. But I wasn't clear on what I was looking for, causing several fits and starts before I began to think about all the things that I loved and wanted to include in my Nxt. With that clarity, I was able to evolve my dream into its next iteration.

And then it evolved even more. I never imagined I'd start from the ground up to create my Nxt dream. I had never built a house before, let alone build out an entire environment with animals and a garden. But as I allowed myself to be open to the possibilities, new opportunities began to present themselves, and we found the property that would ultimately become the foundation for my Nxt.

It's common to start out totally convinced that your initial idea for your Nxt is exactly what you want—only to find that the final version you step into has evolved beyond it.

It's common to start out totally convinced that your initial idea for your Nxt is exactly what you want—only to find that the final version you step into has evolved beyond it.

Important Takeaways

- Finding Your Nxt is about conjuring up an *ideal* description about what you want your Nxt to *do for you*.

- Make a mental list of the ways you've thrived in the past.

- Expand your thinking from what you've been comfortable doing in the past to designing an ideal way of living and working.

- Don't get hung up on the details. Visualize the *big picture* of what you want to achieve.

- Close your eyes, take a deep breath, and imagine what your dream would look and feel like if you could design it to be everything you want it to be.

- Paint a picture in your mind of what you *see*. No blockers getting in your way. No details about how you'd do it. Just a wide-open description of the big picture of what life could be.

- Rarely is the first iteration of your dream the one you end up pursuing.

- You'll know it when you *see* it. Don't limit your possibilities. Sometimes starting from the ground up to create something totally new can be just what you've been looking for.

5

Find Alignment

CHAPTER 5

Find Alignment

If your heart, head, and gut are
telling you the same thing,
then you owe it to yourself to chase it.

—MARC BLUCAS
Riley Finn on *Buffy the Vampire Slayer*

Not long after we closed on the land, my mom, Del, decided it was time to go be with my dad, Paul, who had passed away six years earlier. She had never been the same after he was gone. She hadn't been well physically, but that wasn't the real reason she died. Del died because she couldn't live without her Paul anymore. They were one of those couples who had that fairy-tale kind of relationship. They met when she was 16 and he was 17. Their lives had been intertwined in every way for over fifty years, so when my dad died, it left a gaping hole in Del's heart, a hole so wide and deep that nothing else could fill it. Not friends, not family, not even watching her beloved New York Yankees on TV or spending hours talking politics with my brother. She just wanted to be with her Paul. We all knew living without him for much longer was just not going to work for her.

I found my mama early one morning lying peacefully in her bed, as the light streamed down on her from the bedroom window. She had *the most* serene smile on her face—I knew she had seen her Paul, and they were together again. As sad as I was with the loss of my mom, my heart warmed more than I can express (even as my heart broke more than I could have known possible) now that they were both gone. It was really difficult for me to realize I had now lost both of my parents. They were too young when they died (both were in their 70s), and we still had so many things we wanted to do together.

I had followed them to Colorado when I was 19, from our home in Michigan, because they were making *their* Nxt life change (obviously the apple did not fall far from that tree) and I didn't want to be left out. We liked being a part of each other's lives, and they had always been a huge influence in my life and my success. I knew it was going to be really difficult to figure out this Nxt chapter of my life without my mom and dad right there with me.

I had only recently purchased the property in Ridgway when my mom passed, and my brother, Buddy, hadn't had a chance to see it yet. We had always known our parents had planned to have their ashes spread together *somewhere* in the state, their one caveat being that it had to have gorgeous views (again, apple/tree), but we hadn't discussed *where* that should be. The more I thought about it, the more *obvious* I thought the Ridgway property would be perfect as their final resting place—those gorgeous views having something to do with it. But more importantly (and selfishly perhaps?), I thought it would be incredibly special to have them on the property, close to me.

I decided to talk with Buddy about it. When I suggested we scatter their ashes there, he agreed—sight unseen. I appreciated that he trusted me on this, but there was a part of me that was unsure if I was doing the right thing. What if I was being selfish by putting my need to have them close to *me* ahead of what *they* would have wanted? This land was about *my* Nxt. It didn't represent my parents' lives. What if I was making a huge mistake by suggesting they be laid to rest on a piece of property they had never seen?

Still, my heart was telling me to keep going because it was the right thing to do.

On the day after Mom's memorial, our little extended family— all eleven of us, including Ally and A.J.; Buddy, his wife, Sara, and two kids, Susan and David; two of my closest cousins (Carol and Marcialee); Brian; and my BFF, Nancy—loaded into my RV and took the six-hour drive from Boulder to Ridgway, going directly to the property. The RV bumped and tipped dramatically from side to side as I drove along the old cow path onto the property. I pulled up to a flat spot near where I imagined our house would be one day, and everyone piled out to a chorus of "Ooohs" and "Ahhhs" as they took their first steps on the land and looked out at the magnificent mountain views surrounding us.

I looked over at Buddy. As I watched his gaze sweep over the landscape, he looked back at me, smiled, and nodded his head in warm approval.

I instantly began to relax.

We didn't have a plan for where or how we'd spread their ashes. There was no service written or outline of who would speak or what we'd do for a ceremony. But it all seemed to unfold in a way that made it feel natural and right. A.J. pointed to a couple of old cottonwood trees near the middle of the property and suggested they might offer a great spot for the ceremony. As we approached the trees, you could see that one was significantly larger than the other, and its branches were almost protectively hanging over the smaller tree—just like my dad would have done with my mom.

My dad (Poppy to the grandkids) was a big man who towered over my mom (Grammy), who was a tiny woman. Whenever they were together in a group, they would stand side-by-side, either holding hands or Paul having his arm draped over Del's shoulders. It wasn't just a gesture we noticed once in a while; it was the thing they always did that demonstrated the connection between them. They were inseparable. So when Ally said, "Those trees look like Grammy and Poppy standing together waiting for us," those two cottonwoods became, and would forever be, referred to as *the grandparent trees.*

The grandparent trees had grown close together over time, with their branches and leaves forming a thick canopy above a naturally forming circle below, which was covered with a bed of fallen leaves. The breeze was picking up, and the clouds were beginning to roll in (the weather can change so fast in Colorado), pushing us all to stand under the canopy as a natural protection from the incoming weather. Once under the tree limbs, we decided to use the opening between the base of the two trees to spread my parents' ashes together and protect them from the elements.

A.J. began our ad hoc ceremony by reciting one of the poems he had written, which was both appropriate for the occasion and a favorite of Grammy's. Buddy told several funny (and tender) stories about our parents, and the rest of us joined in with more stories and family legends, reminiscing and laughing until we couldn't laugh anymore.

With the "ceremony" coming to an end, A.J. and Buddy's son, David, began spreading Del and Paul's ashes together in a circle—keeping them intertwined for all time—as we all raised our glasses and toasted the lives of our parents, grandparents, aunt and uncle, and friends. We all felt so good being there together. It all felt so right, and yet, deep in my gut I still had a nagging question haunting me: Is this what *my parents* would have wanted?

And then it began to rain.

We were all still huddled together under the canopy of the grandparent trees when my niece, Susan, looked to the south and suddenly said, "Oh my goodness. Everyone, look!" She pointed. "There's a double rainbow." We all looked up, and there was a collective gasp. Before our eyes was a perfectly formed, full double rainbow on the horizon.

It had to be a sign.

No one made a sound for several minutes until Buddy said, "Well, I guess it's pretty clear that Del and Paul approve of being here for all time." Everybody let out a collective sigh.

Then, as if on cue, everyone looked at me.

I was standing there with tears streaming down my face, staring at the rainbow. Then I started bawling. All of the emotion poured out of me. Ally quickly moved over and threw her arms around me. Then A.J. put his arms around both of us, and the whole damn family came over to form a huge group hug. We could all feel Del and Paul with us in that moment.

It was perfect.

I hadn't really cried with everyone before that (I had been on autopilot, taking care of all the details and making all of the arrangements), but as soon as I saw that double rainbow spread across the sky, I finally released all the fear, the loss, the anxiety, and the selfishness I had bottled up inside of me.

I had no idea I was waiting for a sign. And let's be clear: I had *no* idea that the sign I was waiting for was their approval about spreading their ashes on the land, as well as their approval about my getting the land in the first place.

That double rainbow provided me with both.[*]

Up until the rainbow sign, I logically knew I was making a good decision about this piece of land. It was a kick-ass deal for a stunning piece of property that provided me a ton of opportunities to build a future. My head was feeling very confident about my choice, and my heart was filled with an overwhelming sense of joy every time I stood on it and gazed out at the magnificent views surrounding it.

But my parents had always been my gut check. And I was feeling a void in my decision-making process without that. They had an uncanny sense of where the potential pitfalls were buried and would always point them out so I could avoid them. They were my backup alarm system. Without that safeguard in my life, I wasn't

---

[*] Don't you think we all need some approval when we're making a really big life change? I certainly did. My approval just happened to be a super-cool double rainbow at my parents' ash-spreading ceremony, which I took be a giant A-OK sign from both Del and Paul. No big deal.

sure I had a strong-enough gut to warn me if something was about to go wrong.

That sign made me realize what had been nagging at me: I hadn't felt aligned in my head, my heart, and my gut about my decision. My head had been onboard, and my heart was as happy as hell, but my gut needed to know all was clear through my parents' approval. (The alternative sign would have been a torrential windstorm with hail pummeling through the tree canopy, by the way.)

Once I knew my gut was good, I became fully aligned for what was Nxt.

Sigh.

The family spent the rest of the afternoon walking the land and exploring all of its little unique areas before heading to a local hotel for the rest of the night. Once there and settled in for the evening, we gathered in my hotel room, where I described the vision I had for the property. I hadn't seen it quite as clearly before that day, but with my parents nestled safely on the property, I was able to paint a picture of the land's future for all of my loved ones to see.

Not only could I see it, but now, so could they.

Achieving Alignment

Confusion can easily set into decision-making when your rational thinking (your head), your purpose and values (your heart), and your built-in danger detector (your gut) aren't aligned. It's normal to have internal conversations with ourselves about information we need or concerns we have. Paying attention to what your head is asking for, what your heart needs, and any red flags your gut is spotting is so important when making major decisions. Ignoring the internal conversations that happen inside your head, heart, and gut will usually lead to either going offtrack, hitting a roadblock, or becoming unable to move forward on your path entirely.

> *Paying attention to what your head is asking for, your heart needs, and any red flags your gut is spotting is so important when making major decisions.*

Your head is where your logic and rationale come from to help you make decisions. It wants data. It wants to know what information and knowledge will justify any action you take. It's logical and rational, requiring answers to questions before you make a choice. Listen to your head. It will raise questions needing answers before you make a final decision to move forward. Identify the unknowns and fill in the missing pieces so your head has what it needs to be confident with your decision.

Your heart is the home for your purpose and values. If you feel your heart ache (I swear you can actually *feel* it), ask yourself: What's worrying you? What concerns do you have? Your heart will feel horrible if your actions are misaligned with your values and purpose.

Conversely, did you know you can *feel* your heart get excited when you are faced with a choice that will serve you best? Listen (and feel) for that pitter-patter of your heart, and if you feel it, keep moving forward in your exploration. Your heart is your guide to feeling good about moving in one direction or another. If you listen to your heart, you'll be able to know if your Nxt is something you will value, if it will satisfy you—or make you happy—and any of the other zillion positive things an opportunity can provide to you.

Your gut is your warning system. Your gut is able to see what your head and heart might miss, because it's a pro at reading between the lines. It has the capacity to hit you in the face with red flags, scream alarms in your head, or point to the pitfalls hidden in the road ahead of you.

Your gut can also provide you the most soothing inner glow if there are calm seas in front of you. Pay attention to your gut when it's quiet; it means you are free to continue moving in the direction you are headed. But when your gut is reacting with alarm, recognize that something may be wrong or will require your attention before you move ahead.

Your head, heart, and gut are the trifecta of tools within your personal tool kit for decision-making. If one is off, pay attention, slow down, and explore what's off. But if all three are aligned, be assured you are going down the best path toward your Nxt.

Doubting Yourself

There might be times when figuring out what's Nxt that you doubt yourself and your ability to make the changes or decisions to move forward. It's natural and expected. If this happens, it's best to look at whether there are any missing pieces of information you need to gain the confidence to move forward with your decision. Are your head, heart, and gut all in alignment? Do you have what you need to move forward? Do your values align with what you are doing? Is your gut sounding any alarms, or is it calm and quiet? It's important to make sure you are gathering all the information you need to feel more confident with every decision you make as you find your Nxt.

After my mom passed and my brother and I knew we had to find a special place to have the ceremony for my parents, my head was telling me the property *was* that special place. Logically, it all made sense. I had just purchased a beautiful piece of property in the mountains, with gorgeous views, and *I knew* that if my parents had been able to see it, they would have loved it.

My heart was onboard as well. Everything about the property and the potential of the kind of life I thought I could live there filled my heart with joy. I wanted my family to see it and experience what I felt when I was there, so bringing them to the property to spread my parents' ashes on-site would fill my heart and theirs too.

So why the heck was I so worried about spreading my parents' ashes on the property? I *knew* it was the perfect place, but I kept doubting myself every step of the way.

Because my gut was unsure.

There were gaps in my information and questions I needed to have answered about things I valued most *before* I could feel completely confident about my decision. Without filling in those gaps and getting the answers I needed, I couldn't be completely sure I was doing the right thing, and I would continue to doubt myself.

First, I needed to know whether my brother felt the same way I did about having our parents' ashes on the property. I valued his opinion and feelings so much that without knowing he was fully onboard, I couldn't be sure of my decision. I also didn't want him to think I was being selfish. Even though they were only ashes (and not really *our parents*) I didn't want him thinking I was hogging them. (I know—it's a younger-sibling insecurity thing.) But once he gave me his nod of approval, I knew in my heart it was the right move, and I was able to back away from all that crazy, insecure stuff.

Second, I needed some sign that my parents *would have* approved of the decision to spread their ashes on the property—and I needed a sense of approval from them that I'd made a good decision about buying the property in the first place. Whether or not that double rainbow was *actually* a sign of their approval wasn't the question. I *believed* it was (and apparently so did the rest of my family). That was enough to make me feel I had made the right decision.

Your heart is your guide to feeling good about moving in one direction or another.

Finally, up until the ceremony, the people who were most important to me hadn't stepped foot on the property. I had shared with all of them a bit about my ideas for this Nxt chapter of my life, but until they could see it for themselves, I don't think they understood the scale and nature of the change I was about to embark upon. Once I was able to lay out my vision and paint a picture of the future I wanted them to be a part of, the missing pieces started to fall in place, and a lot of my questions (and theirs) were answered. When that happened, my gut settled down, and I released a lot of my doubts.

Understanding how important alignment is, as each decision presents itself, is fundamental to successfully moving forward into your dream. Use the built-in tool kit you have at your disposal to help steer you through the morass of information, decisions, and approvals you'll need on your journey.

As you navigate the process of figuring out what's Nxt, new challenges constantly arise, forcing you to gain more clarity and focus in order to make each decision you face. Provide your head with all of the information it needs. Check in with your heart to make sure it's going pitter-pat and not feeling heartsick. And trust your gut. If it's slapping you in the face with red flags—pay attention. Something's not quite right, and it's worth slowing down to find out what.

Important Takeaways

⬦ Confusion can affect decision-making when your rational thinking (your head), your purpose and values (your heart), and your built-in danger detector (your gut) aren't aligned.

⬦ Your head is your rational and logical tool that helps you decide.

⬦ If your head has questions, go out and fill in the gaps with the information it needs to decide.

⬦ Your heart is the home of your purpose and values.

⬦ Your heart can ache when things aren't right, and it can go pitter-pat when it's excited about the direction you're headed.

⬦ Follow your heart when you want to abide by your values, be satisfied with what you are doing, and become happy in your life.

⬦ Your gut is your warning system.

⬦ Your gut will hit you in the face with red flags, get all upset when it sees pitfalls ahead, and scream loud alarms when faced with something that could go wrong.

⬦ Pay attention to your gut.

⬦ Your head, heart, and gut are the trifecta of tools within your personal tool kit for decision-making.

⬦ When your head, heart, and gut are aligned, you can be confident that your decision is right-on.

⬦ The next time you see a double rainbow, I hope you'll think of my parents.

6

Define What's Important

CHAPTER 6

Define What's Important

Anything less than a conscious commitment to
the important is an unconscious commitment
to the unimportant.

—STEPHEN COVEY
American educator and author

I t was finally time to begin envisioning the kind of house that would be center stage for this Nxt stage of life. Exciting? Absolutely! And yet, I had no idea how to build a house from the ground up. I had no idea how to start the process. Actually, I had no idea how to begin just about everything else, because everything about this life was new. *All of it.*

Not just the house. The whole place. The land. The location. The openness. The freedom. There were so many ways we could do this. This place was a blank slate. It was open pasture. No driveway.

No services. No blueprint. We were free to design the house any way we wanted, put it anywhere we wanted, and dream about how we wanted to live in and around it for many years to come.

This was exciting—and daunting.

Most people will tell you the first thing you need to do when building a house is to lay out the basics. How many bedrooms do you want? Bathrooms? Kitchen layout? Open floor plan or more traditional room layout? One- or two-car garage? In other words, define your house in terms of its *functionality*—which is important and ultimately necessary to getting what you want. But this house was only the *first* building of what we knew was a much larger plan for the property, so we had to think bigger and more long-term.

Having your own personal Big Why statement provides you a filter for decision-making.

We had to think differently.

We weren't just building a house; we were building a new life. So we needed to take time to focus on what was *really important* for us in building this house and in creating our dream lifestyle.

Matthew and I talked for hours about all of it. We dreamed alone and we dreamed together. Slowly, we began to form a list of what we wanted this new life to *do* for us. What was important in the spaces we wanted to create? How did we want others to be with us on the property? What was important about how we would live our lives here? What did we want this place to *feel* like?

Here's how the list ended up:

1. We want to take advantage of all the views around us and incorporate the natural surroundings into everything we do, but also create living spaces that will feel protected from the elements, providing safety and warmth.

2. We know this is a special place—one that needs to be shared with others. We recognize that we will be living six hours (by car) from our family and friends, so they won't be dropping by. So not only will we need to accommodate guests in our main house, but we'll also need to build separate guest accommodations that will be welcoming, comfortable, and close by, but not on top of us so everyone can have their own space.

3. We want our main house to feel like it expands to be open and comfortable with a large group of people who are visiting, and yet contracts to be warm and cozy enough when it's just Matthew and me.

4. We envision living a sustainable lifestyle utilizing reusable and renewable energy, sustainable building products, and local materials and contractors. This is important to our values, and it embodies our dream for the way we want to live into the future.

5. We also want to be self-sustaining as much as possible. This means growing our own food (both animal and vegetable) and creating income sources that will allow us to build our lifestyle over time.

6. We want to dance! Matthew and I met when he was my dance instructor, and dancing continues to be a big part of our relationship. So we need to incorporate a space within our house to dance, for and by ourselves, and for and with others.

7. We want to create a place to experience life—not just live day-to-day. So there will always need to be ways to involve people in how we live.

8. We want the process of designing and building out the property to be fun—fun for us and fun for everyone who will be involved. We know if we set out to make it fun, then fun will be imbued in the bones of everything we build, and that will be felt by everyone who comes here.

9. We feel a responsibility for the land and intend to be caretakers of it. We want all of our buildings and activities to blend into the surroundings, while adding interest, dimension, and practicality to the use of the land.

10. We want to maximize the potential of this time and space—for our life now and for our legacy into the future.

These ten concepts were nonnegotiable. They were bigger than the components of the house. They were the foundation of the life we were intending to create. They were a fundamental part of this Nxt dream of ours.

They became our *Big Why* for doing all of this.

Using Our *Big Why*

When looking for an architect, we used our *Big Why* statement to help determine who would be the right fit, who would *get it*, and who would get us. Nowhere on the statement did it indicate how many bedrooms or bathrooms were required. Nor did it define what kind of kitchen or family room we wanted to create. It didn't specify the style or finishes of the house. Instead, it spelled out everything that was most important to us about *how* we wanted to live, which we knew would be a confusing and uncomfortable language for most architects to comprehend.

One architect looked at the list and told us to come back when we figured out the type and style of house we wanted to build, and then he could design that. Another told us that we needed to be specific about the kind of floor plan we wanted and the number of bedrooms and baths before he'd talk to us again. For a while, it wasn't going very well. In total we talked with five architects and *only one*, Jeff, got it.

I met Jeff at a small coffee shop in Boulder. We sat outside, and I handed him the ten-point list across the little round table. He took a few minutes to read it, looked up at me, and said, "OK, so I think you've just given me a mission statement for your house—which I don't think I've ever gotten from a client before.

"But I like it," he continued. "It's helping me get a feeling for how you want to live there."

Yes! He got it. Now we needed to find out if he could really *see* it.

A few weeks later, we met Jeff on the property and sat together in three folding chairs, just taking in the view. After several minutes, Jeff leaned back and said, "Sitting here, on this land with the views in front of me, I can certainly understand *why* you love this place and why it's so important for you to live the way you described."

He continued, "I can see a whole bunch of ways to design what you want."

Yes again! It was exciting (and a bit of a relief) to know that someone else could see it.

I nodded calmly and smiled. (I really wanted to jump up and down, but I didn't want to show my excitement too much because we were still "interviewing" him.) He kept looking out at the view until he turned to us and said, "Man, if you'd have me, I'd love to work with you to make this dream come true."

At that point, I did jump up and thrust out my hand. Instead of shaking it, Jeff pulled me into a hug, and we knew we were now in this together.

We went through the same process in finding a builder. We talked with five different contractors. Four of them challenged several concepts within the mission statement and the accompanying plans, without offering any suggestions or alternatives. The contractor we chose spread out our plans, set our mission statement list beside it, and said, "OK, you seem to know what you want and why, so let's see how we can meet all your needs in a way that will also meet your budget."

Yes! We hired that guy too.

What Is Your *Big Why*?

Most businesses have mission statements to help align their workforce toward a common set of principles and goals. In the same

way, being able to articulate your own personal *Big Why* helps
to clarify and align the principles and values by which you'll live
your life. Regardless of whether your Nxt is about your lifestyle,
your work, or your relationship, having clarity about *what matters
most to you* is invaluable as you move through
the process. Our natural tendency is to begin
with a more tactical approach when seeking
something new. However, if you identify what
is most important to you *first*, you'll gain a
sense of certainty right out of the gate about
what you'll *need to have* in order to succeed, be
happy, and be fulfilled in your Nxt.

For my Nxt, the big change began with my
lifestyle, so when it was time to start planning
our house, practical wisdom told us to start
with functionality: how many bedrooms and
bathrooms, etc. But we couldn't do that without first determining what was most important about how we wanted to *actually live* on
the Ranch. That required us to create a list of
concepts that would end up being so important that they became our guiding principles
for how we would run the entire operation on
the Ranch.

*Here's the thing:
If you're going to
take the time and
make the effort to
step into your Nxt,
don't you think
it should meet
as many of the
criteria of what's
most important to
you as possible?*

Our *Big Why* became the framework on which we built the
entirety of our Nxt. We used it to clarify our purpose, to articulate
our intentions, and to list the things that were most important to
us as we designed, defined, and developed our new life. It became
the most valuable and fundamental tool we had throughout the

entire development of the Ranch. It is something we still refer to years later.

What's *Most* Important to You

As I've worked with clients over the years, I've learned how crucial a concise list of "What's *Most* Important to You" is when helping each individual move into their Nxt. When clients come to the Ranch for my Immersion program to find their Nxt, I often have them do an exercise the first evening: They list *all the things* they believe are important to them about working, their most significant relationship, and their lifestyle. I ask them not to hold back. I want them to vomit out all the words that represent everything they believe is important to them—to any degree.

First we concentrate on what is important about *the way they work*. Notice I don't ask them to list their criteria for doing a specific job. Instead, I ask for them to list the ways they would *thrive while working*. It's a totally different perspective, one that shifts them from focusing on tasks they're proficient at (which we come back to later) to thinking about *how* they work best.

When making a list about their *relationship*, I ask them to put aside any individual behaviors about a specific person and use words that describe what is important to them about *being in a relationship*. This forces them to think more expansively about what they expect from an ideal relationship, based on their needs and wants.

The same holds true for their list of what's most important about their *lifestyle*. I ask them to think beyond their current living situation and define what would be most important to have if they were living their *ideal* life.

The next morning, we review their lists and consolidate them into what's *most* important in each of the three categories. I have them explain each word, and then we begin to combine, adjust, and prioritize—reducing their list to about five or six key concepts in each category. Once we have that key list completed and they believe each word honestly represents them, we combine the three lists into a comprehensive outline of their most important principles for working, for being in a relationship, and for the life they want to live. It represents their *Big Why*— including all of their must-haves for making decisions in any of those areas of life.

Having your own personal *Big Why* statement provides you a filter for decision-making. It becomes your checklist to bounce decisions against to see if an opportunity passes muster or not. If you are looking to change careers, you have a list of the most important criteria for any new work you do. If you can check the boxes, great! If you can't, then you can choose to compromise, or you can say "no" and continue your search until you find a job that reflects the values that are most important to you.

Do the same thing when deciding about a relationship or anything to do with a change in your lifestyle. If it checks your boxes, then it's an easy "yes." If it doesn't, then it's either a deal-breaker, or you can *intentionally* move ahead, knowing that you are making a compromise by giving up something on your list. The point is that you'll know your baseline so you're able to make a conscious decision.

Here's the thing: Your *Big Why* is meant to be a *Big Deal*. It's meant to force you to take a hard look before you jump into a decision. It's designed to clearly define the most important things to *you*, in order to make it really difficult to give those things up. It's *your* list, so you can make exceptions and compromises all you want, but by having a clear list in front of you, you'll know what you're moving away from and why. And if the criteria outlined in your *Big Why* statement are truly important to you, you won't make frivolous decisions. Knowing your *Big Why* gives you crystal clarity on why you're moving forward in a certain direction, and it takes you far down the road to finding your Nxt.

Hard Yes, Easy No

Most of us have an easier time saying yes than no. We tend to want to be accommodating and nice and thoughtful, and it can feel hard to say no. Often, we will push aside whatever might be important to us in favor of a request from someone else, because we don't want to let them down or put them in a bind or because it feels good to help. I get it. Saying no is hard, so saying yes becomes easy by default.

Having a list of what is most important to you—and holding it to be sacred—is the only way to move from the *Easy* Yes/*Hard* No to the *Hard* Yes/*Easy* No. I'm not talking about becoming a selfish, rude, or bitchy person who, because they know what's important to them, totally negates what's important to someone else. I'm talking about recognizing that what's *most important to you* should have tremendous weight when making important decisions that will lead you to your Nxt.

Here's the thing: If you're going to take the time and make the effort to step into your Nxt, don't you think it should meet as many of the criteria of what's most important to you as possible? Shouldn't all of those boxes be checked for you to be able to say yes? And if those boxes aren't checked, don't you want to get to the easy no and be able to move on?

For example, you want to make a career change and find a position that appeals to you. You successfully move through the interview process and get a job offer, but it's not what you were hoping for. The work won't capitalize on your skills, you won't be doing the kind of work you had hoped to do, and the money isn't really enough. You could say yes because you got the offer and it would be easier to take the job and stop your search, but in less than six months you'll probably end up miserable and feeling like you had settled for something less than what was really important to you. Or, you can say no (the obvious answer), because the job offer doesn't meet your criteria for what is really important to you.

Knowing what's important to you takes the guesswork out of decisions. The "no" becomes easier (and a lot more obvious) and the "yes" becomes harder, because you know what you need and are willing to set the bar that high for yourself.

Here's an example of an Easy No: "I can't take that job because it doesn't meet my conditions for working in a leadership position, with room to grow, at the salary I believe I've earned through my work experience."

Conversely, here's when you know it's in your best interest to say yes: You receive a job offer that is *exactly* what you've been looking for. You'll have the opportunity to lead a team, there is room for growth, and they've exceeded your compensation requirements. Woo-hoo! Everything that is most important to you has been met. It might have seemed harder to get there, but you checked your boxes, and now the "yes" seems easy because you had clarity about what you needed to move forward.

Can I Say Yes Without Checking All the Boxes?

If you choose to move forward with a Nxt step that doesn't check all of your boxes, then do so intentionally. That's OK. There are certainly times when circumstances dictate that it is more prudent to start with a partial list checked off and work toward adding the other important concepts down the road, but it must be an intentional act.

Your list can also morph over time. Different times of our lives, different phases, and changing circumstances can change what is most important to us. If a loved one needs your support, or the needs of your job change, or your life partner has an opportunity that would change your living situation for the time being, then you might have to amend or adjust something on your previous list. But if you do so, recognize that you're probably doing it because it addresses something else that is even more important to you at that time.

When we created our *Big Why* statement at the beginning of our Nxt, it became our foundational guidebook for making decisions throughout the process of building out the Ranch. As we built the house and all of the outbuildings, we used it to help keep us on track and guide us in our decision-making. Whether it was choosing building materials, deciding whether an investment in an outbuilding was worthwhile, or figuring out how to monetize the Ranch to keep our lifestyle going, having a list of what was most important made the no's easier and helped us scrutinize our yes's—holding everything to our highest standards—while helping us make the best decisions along the way.

Important Takeaways

⋄ A personal *Big Why* statement helps you clarify and align the principles and values by which you define the life you *really* want to live.

⋄ A concise list of "What's *Most* Important to You" is crucial to helping you move into your Nxt.

⋄ Create your own personal *Big Why* statement, including your *must-haves* for thriving while working, being in a relationship, and living your ideal life.

⋄ Make your list a declaration of what you are unwilling to compromise.

⋄ Move from the *Easy* Yes/*Hard* No to the *Hard* Yes/*Easy* No.

⋄ Your list can morph over time. That's OK. Circumstances change.

⋄ For God's sake, if you're ever going to build *anything*, find an architect who's willing to spend time with you to talk through the possibilities and can see your vision—and appreciates the *Big Why* you've laid out.

7

Naming CC Blue

CHAPTER 7

Naming CC Blue

*. . . for to name a thing is to give it
order and purpose . . .*

—N.K. JEMISIN
The Hundred Thousand Kingdoms

Being a girl who grew up with the TV westerns of the '60s and '70s—watching the Ponderosa on *Bonanza* and the Barkley Ranch on *The Big Valley*—I wanted to name our property and have folks refer to our place as the "_____ Ranch." It felt important. In fact, a lot of the ranches and farms around us had names like the Horsefly Mesa Ranch, The Lazy L Ranch, and even Ralph Lauren's Double RL (RRL), named for him and his wife, Ricky.

As I did a little digging around, it seemed like there were several ways to name a piece of property. It could be a description of where the ranch was located, as in the Horsefly Mesa Ranch, which sat below Horsefly Mesa. Or it could follow the standards of traditional livestock branding and receive a *real cattle brand* through the Department of Agriculture—made up of a whole language of letters, digits, and symbols dating back to the late 1800s. Or you could make up a name out of thin air and call it whatever the hell you wanted—which was the way I did things.

If you didn't name your property, however, the name would most likely default to the surname of the original owner (most recently or dating *waaaaaay* back to the original owner). So the ranch would always be referred to as "the Old Hansen Place" even though everyone on the planet knew you weren't part of the Old Hansen family. (Which would drive me crazy!)

So we decided we had to name our ranch so we could call it something other than "Our Ranch" or the Old Hansen Place.

Over lunch one day, sitting in the RV on the property while construction was in full swing around us, Matthew and I threw out a number of names that had us rolling our eyes, fake gagging, or laughing out loud: *Casa Carrillo, Mountains Gate, Peaceful Ranch, Happy Days Ranch, Tango Farm, Two Step Ranch, Dreamy Acres,* and many more came flying out of our mouths. Each was too cutesy, too kitschy, or too stupid. Obviously, we had never named a piece of property before.

Then Matthew unintentionally moved his phone on the table and his list of recent calls lit up, showing the name "CC Blue" at the top. I looked at the phone and then at him. I said, "Who's that?" (Using a tone that was inadvertently accusatory.)

He laughed and said, "It's *you,* silly! That's how I have you listed in my phone."

I never knew that.

Matthew had started calling me "Blue" early in our relationship, because I have blue eyes (sigh). The CC was for my initials. (How sweet was that?) I was really touched and leaned over to kiss him for the heartwarming gesture, but as I moved away, he pulled me back and whispered, "How about we call this place 'CC Blue'?"

"What?" I said. "Wouldn't that be a little selfish on my part?" *And arrogant and say to the world that I was full of myself,* I thought.

He smiled tenderly. "I think it's perfect. It's personal, but not too obvious, and I think it fits this place—and you."

CC Blue. We said it over and over.

And he was right.

It fit this place—and me—perfectly.

Important Takeaways

❖ Properties of a certain size get named. It's a thing.

❖ Naming your property can be like naming your kid. It's intense.

❖ If your significant other has a sweet nickname for you that includes the color of your eyes, you might want to keep him or her around for a long time.

8

Live with Intention

CHAPTER 8

Live with Intention

Dance is like dreaming with your feet.

—CONSTANZE MOZART
Singer who was once married to Wolfgang Mozart

uring Christmas a number of years *before* I sold the company (and when Brian and I were still married), he gave me a card that read, "I want you to follow your love of dance and take ballroom lessons," followed by, "Really, go for it. Merry Christmas." He knew I was aching to fulfill my dream of getting out on a dance floor to *dance backward in heels* the way Ginger Rogers did (or at least as well as I could). It wasn't a typical Brian gift, and I thought it was an incredibly sweet and thoughtful thing for him to do. However, *he* had absolutely no desire to take dance lessons *with me*. OK. Not the way I would have set it up, but it was still incredibly sweet and thoughtful, and he was right. I *was* aching to learn how to ballroom dance.

Since I would be going it alone, we agreed I would look for a group ballroom class with like-minded strangers who were interested in learning how to foxtrot and waltz (frontward and backward) with other solo dancers. How difficult could that be?

For weeks I looked everywhere for group lessons but couldn't find anything. Frustrating, because you'd think there would be other solo dancers looking for a group to dance with, but it wasn't as common as I had thought. Still, I persisted.

As I continued my search, I stumbled upon a local ballroom dance studio that advertised group lessons. I excitedly placed a call. The owner answered the phone.

"Hi," I said. "I'm looking to take some group dance lessons and was wondering if you had anything available at this time."

"Yes," she said. "We have them, but you don't want to take group lessons. You want to take private lessons with Matthew because he's the best. Taking privates with him is really the only way to go."

"Hmmm," I said. "That's cool, but no thanks. I only want to take group lessons. When do those classes meet?"

"No, really," she said. "You don't want to take a group class. You want to take private lessons with Matthew."

"Noooo," I repeated. I only want—" and then she interrupted me.

"Oh, there he is on the other line now. I'll have him call you."

And she hung up.

I stared at the phone.

Who the heck did this woman think she was? I wanted to take group lessons, so I was going to take group lessons. *Damn it!*

And who the heck was this Matthew guy, anyway?

I had no interest in talking to a guy who was going to try to sell me private dance lessons.

As incredulous as I was with that whole conversation and the fact that she *threatened* (OK, maybe too strong a word, but it kind of felt like it) to have that instructor call me, I put the phone down and decided to continue my search because—let's be honest—what were the odds that this guy Matthew would call me back?

Ten minutes later the phone rang.

It was Matthew. And he was totally charming.

In the first two minutes, he proved to be very knowledgeable about the art of teaching dance and made me feel like he *really* wanted to teach me. When I tried to politely tell him I would prefer to take group lessons, he began to (smoothly) convince me that, *in my case*, private lessons would be far superior to group lessons. "You'll get the kind of attention *you deserve* in a private lesson," he said. "And the progress you'll make in *just a few lessons* will be far greater than anything you'd be able to achieve in a group." (I could feel myself softening—actually *melting*—to the idea.)

> *It was Matthew. And he was totally charming.*

And then he dropped the big hook to reel me in. "And I'm running a three-hour introductory special for private lessons this month."

Damn it! I love a good sale.

So I signed up.

The whole call took six and a half minutes, and I was in—hook, line, and sinker.

I arrived for my three hours of dancing on the Saturday following our call, with two huge bottles of water in my hand, one for me and one for Matthew (because *I* was raised never to arrive anywhere empty-handed). He took his huge bottle of water and thanked me with a confused look on his face, because (unbeknownst to me) no one had *ever* brought him anything for a lesson before. (Obviously, his other students had been raised in caves.)

We spent the next hour dancing some foxtrot, waltz, cha-cha, swing, and salsa. It was meant to give me a taste of all the different genres of dance to see what fit me best, and what we might want to concentrate on moving forward. I sucked at most of them, but it was glorious. I loved every minute of it.

After an hour of dancing, Matthew said, "OK, that's it for today." I looked at him, confused. "Wait," I said. "I thought I had three hours as part of the special?"

He laughed. "Not *all* in one lesson," he said. "The special is for three *one-hour* lessons."

Ah. I felt like an idiot (and clearly the *huge* bottle of water was overkill). But he didn't make me feel stupid. He simply asked, "So when would you like to come back for your next lessons?"

"Tomorrow," I said. "And the day after that, if you're available."

Those first few hours turned into lessons once or twice a week for the next couple of years and expanded into a full-blown obsession for me about learning how to dance.

After Brian and I divorced, Matthew and I ended up dating. (I know; I was dating my dance instructor!) Over time we became more and more a part of each other's lives. We were together in a lot of ways, but in many other ways, we still led separate lives. I had my family and business and friends, and he had his. Both of us had been married before, and neither of us wanted to get married again. But the longer we were together, the more the lines separating our lives began to blur, and we became a pretty serious thing.

And then I sold the company.

As I began to dream about the idea of finding a beautiful piece of property in the mountains with a gorgeous view, Matthew was the one I shared it all with. He was a part of the process from that first trip to look at properties with Michelle, through the bidding on the land, choosing the architect, and defining what was most important about creating CC Blue. We did it all side by side.

At no time during that whole process, however, did we ever sit down and have a serious conversation about what we each wanted in terms of *our relationship*, both on and off the Ranch. It felt like we were being swept up in the momentum of it all and we'd never made a conscious choice to do this Nxt together. We were a couple (that was clear), and we appeared to be in this together, but at no time did we make an *intentional decision* to make this Nxt a joint venture. Every time we'd go to CC Blue, we'd talk about our future on the Ranch, using language like "*We* should put a garden over there," or "*We* could have cows on the property and raise our own beef." But *we* hadn't acknowledged whether this was a *Cindy thing* (and Matthew would be a part of it when/if he wanted to) or if this was a Cindy *and* Matthew thing.

We were just going with the flow. Like leaves floating on the water in a meandering stream. I was totally fine with that *until* the Main House was built, furnished, and ready for me to move in. Then it all became real. And the whole "going with the flow thing" started to feel too fluid and directionless. We had hit that

point in finding this Nxt where we needed to have more definition and structure about what we were doing. It was time to stop
momentum from taking us down the stream and intentionally put
our oars in the water and steer in a direction we chose. In rela-
tionship-speak, we needed to make a
commitment one way or the other.

If it was a joint dream, then we
needed to declare it—out loud—and
to each other. If it turned out that it
wasn't, then we needed to redefine
how this Nxt was going to look moving
forward. And that was OK either way.
But everything inside me was telling
me it was time to commit to it, define
it, and declare it out loud, *or* move on in
another direction.

"So," I said to Matthew one fine day,
"I'm curious if you've given any thought
to whether or not you would want to
make this your full-on life with me?"
(Oy—who says, "full-on life"?)

"What do you mean?" he said. (Such
a guy response.)

> *Momentum equals
> movement, which you
> can initiate to create
> the energy to move you
> forward, or momentum
> can be instigated by the
> circumstances around
> you, forcing you to
> move in a direction
> you may or may not
> want to go.*

"You know, leaving Boulder and settling in together at the
Ranch to create this phase of our lives together."

That little interlude was enough to set up the discussion I was
looking for. We talked about the possibilities and concerns we had
with taking this big step together, and under what circumstances
each of us was comfortable leaving Boulder to move to the Ranch,

full-on. We decided to do a *test run* by spending April to August at the Ranch to see how we liked living this version of life together. We agreed to have another discussion on Labor Day to see what we each wanted to do beyond that.

During those five months, we leaned into our momentum. We talked, we planned, and we did a ton of shit around the property. Then, on Labor Day, we had an honest, forthright, and amazing discussion, resulting in our decision to step full-on into this Nxt dream *together*. It was the commitment and intention I was looking for, and what (I knew) we *both* needed to make this *our* thing.

Be Intentional

You can move in a direction intentionally, or you can let momentum take you down the path of least resistance. Intentionality is about deciding to move in *one direction versus another* or *to do* one thing or another, consciously choosing between options. As you find and move into your Nxt, you'll (of course) want to think through all the possibilities, all the different scenarios, and play out all the pros and cons in your mind. But if you want to *do* something, you'll reach a point when you'll need to stop exploring and intentionally decide which option to choose. Otherwise you'll end up either staying exactly where you are, doing what you've been doing—or you'll end up moving down the road *unintentionally* and end up doing what someone else decides.

Indecision is a way of allowing momentum to propel you forward without you intentionally deciding to go that way. Matthew and I could have moved in together at the Ranch without ever intentionally deciding to live together. It could have happened without any discussion and without any intention. How many of us let the momentum of our relationships take us down the path of dating, then spending some nights together, then living together, and ultimately getting married—without a lot of intentionality behind those moves? I hate to say it, but it happens a lot. Sometimes it's because those conversations can be tough to have, but mostly it's because the momentum carrying our relationship along becomes the path of least resistance. It's easier to keep moving with the flow than change course.

Of course, sometimes things work out just fine, even when we're not intentional.

So wait a minute. If you can still move forward without intention, then why be intentional? Why not settle for "fine"?

Because intentionality forces you to become clear on your rationale for making a change *before* you move in one direction versus another. It forces you to think through *why* you want to move ahead, instead of moving ahead simply because you can. Moving to CC Blue full-time was a really important decision in both our lives. And even though we had spent a bunch of time figuring out what was most important to us about building out the Ranch (our *Big Why*), we never stopped (until this point) to intentionally figure out why we should do this Nxt chapter together. We were just *assuming* we'd do it together, without making an intentional decision to move in that direction.

Intentionality is about deciding to move in one direction versus another or to do one thing or another, consciously choosing between options.

But living together (even at our age) was a big deal and a big commitment. I did not want to *unintentionally* start the Nxt chapter of my life that way. I wanted to be really clear about the path I was going to take, which meant I needed to know if this was going to be a Cindy thing or a Cindy *and* Matthew thing. Clearly, we needed to face the question, address it (by testing it out), and set a time frame to make an intentional decision one way or the other.

Happily, we concluded that moving onto the Ranch together was exactly what each of us wanted to do. Once we made that decision, we were able to put a stake in the ground and initiate all of the action steps necessary to move full-on into our life at CC Blue. Matthew sold his place. I rented out my house. By December of that year, we were living full-time on the property, doing our Cindy *and* Matthew thing *intentionally.*

Harnessing the Power of Momentum

Momentum equals movement, which *you can initiate* to create the energy to move you forward, or momentum can be instigated by the circumstances around you, forcing you to move in a direction you may or may not want to go. Regardless of the way it's created, there is an energy that comes with momentum. The trick is to consciously try to create momentum and use it to move you where you want to go, rather than put yourself in a situation where momentum happens to you.

I remember a time when I was married to Brian when he was pretty fed up with the health care system and the disconnect that was occurring between doctors and their patients. (Did I mention Brian was a primary care physician?) He was frustrated with the rise of power within the insurance industry and the way insurers were dictating the protocols for care for his patients.

We were lying in bed one night, and he was telling me about one of his patients and how he had called his insurance company to make sure a particular prescribed treatment would be covered, only to be told by "an insurance clerk who knew absolutely nothing about the practice of medicine" that the treatment was unnecessary and payment would be denied.

He was irate, and I didn't blame him.

So I asked him if this was an isolated experience or something that happened all of the time.

"All of the time," he said, "and I'm sick and tired of it." He paused. "And it seriously makes me question whether I want to practice medicine anymore."

I perked up.

"Does that mean you'd like to make a change?" I asked.

He laughed. "Change to do what? I'm a doctor. That's what I do."

Hmmmmm. I had to walk carefully with this one.

"You'll always be a doctor," I said. "But you can figure out how you want to engage with the medical profession moving forward—and make a change if you want to."

He looked at me. It had never crossed his mind he could do anything besides practice medicine the way he had been doing it—*for years.*

He had been groomed to be a doctor since he was a child. His dad used to call him "Doc." And it was always assumed he'd go to college and then to med school, which is what he did (although there were some twists and turns along the way). So there was a momentum behind his career, which had moved him along to where he was now. But he was no longer satisfied being in that place, and it had never dawned on him to intentionally make a change and shift the momentum (of being a doctor) onto a new path of his choosing.

We ended our conversation, and I rolled over and went to sleep. When I awoke the next morning, I was surprised to see Brian sitting up against the headboard in the same position I had seen him in the night before.

I asked him if he was OK. He turned to me and said, "I've been sitting here all night, trying to imagine how I'd practice medicine differently, and I think I have an idea."

So we talked it through, and Brian ended up intentionally initiating a change in his career, which allowed him to practice medicine in a new way, carrying him forward for years down the road.

When momentum is created intentionally and you're able to harness its energy to propel you toward your goal, it can be exhilarating. When it propels you unintentionally, it can feel like you're out of control. You're forced to move in a direction you may not want to go.

We had momentum on the Ranch leading up to the completion of the Main House and Guest House. There was so much activity going on. Water lines were being put in, foundations were being dug, framing was being completed, and the outline of a living compound was being created. There was movement and energy everywhere you looked. It was easy to get swept up in the excitement. For a while, we rode that energy and harnessed every ounce of the momentum we created to get the initial stage of development completed. That momentum served us. It formed the foundation of CC Blue, and we created more momentum down the road with each new addition to the Ranch. The trick was, and continues to be, to drive the momentum on our terms and not let it dictate our direction.

Put a Stake in the Ground

Have you ever begun a sentence about your dream with "I think I'll probably . . ."?

Here's the deal. A life change doesn't *probably* happen. It happens when you make a declaration that you're going to make it happen. You have to put a stake in the ground and declare that you are going to do it. Whatever it is. Otherwise, you'll keep exploring, researching, and thinking about the possibilities of your dream, without ever being able to 1) make a commitment, or 2) make an action plan to make your dream come true.

I had a coaching client who came up with an amazing idea for a business. He and I worked together for weeks, talking about the services his business would provide, the reasons why he thought the business could be successful, and how he envisioned the company could grow over time. We even played around with names for the company and colors for his website.

But he had his doubts and couldn't quite make a commitment to do it. He would talk about the potential of the company by saying, "I think I could probably make the business work, or get enough clients to meet my income needs, or grow the business over time . . ." which did not reflect a level of seriousness or belief that he could make any of that happen. Soon he hit a point where he needed to do more than talk about potential. He had to make an intentional decision to either pursue the idea and move ahead, or let it go.

After a bit more discussion, he decided to launch his business. Almost immediately he stopped saying, "I think I'll probably . . ." and instead started saying, "I'm going to . . ." And as soon as he declared that out loud, he had a burst of relief and exhilaration—coupled with a healthy increase in his heart rate—because he'd put a stake in the ground and made the decision to do it! But here's the real kicker: When he put a stake in the ground to start his business that day, he was able to make a real plan to move fully into his Nxt.

Important Takeaways

⬧ You can move in a direction intentionally, or let momentum take you down the path of least resistance.

⬧ Intentionality is about deciding to move in *one direction versus another* or *to do* one thing or another, consciously choosing between options.

⬧ Indecision is an unconscious decision to keep you where you are.

⬧ Taking the time to explore all the possibilities is good, but the time will come when you need to decide to *do* something.

⬧ Momentum is not good or bad.

⬧ Momentum equals movement. It can be created intentionally or unintentionally.

⬧ Harnessing momentum that you've created, and riding it in the direction you set out, can be a hell of a lot of fun.

⬧ If you want to make your dream happen, then you have to stop saying, "I think I'll *probably* . . ." and start saying, "I'm going to . . ."

⬧ Put a stake in the ground and decide to step into your Nxt.

⬧ If you are in a wonderful relationship but have not made a commitment to take the Nxt step together, don't allow momentum to take you further down the road. Be intentional and decide to move ahead—or not.

9

Bring Your Life with You

CHAPTER 9

Bring Your Life with You

*You learn something valuable from all of the
significant events and people, but you never
touch your true potential until you challenge
yourself to go beyond imposed limitations.*

—ROY T. BENNETT
The Light in the Heart

When we finally completed and moved into our finished house at CC Blue, it really started to hit me: I had moved to a thirty-five-acre ranch without *ever* having spent a day of my life ranching or farming. What was I thinking? I'd never spent my summers on Grandma's farm (because she didn't have a farm). No hanging out at the local stables working with horses. No picking veggies at the local farm, and, to be perfectly honest, only recently discovering that I could purchase veggies from a local farmers market. My farming experience boiled down to a couple of small garden plots in the backyard and the occasional trip to a petting farm with my kids to see, feed, and pet goats and pigs. And let's be very clear: My ranching experience was nonexistent.

So what *was* I thinking?

When I bought the property, I *may or may not* have romantically imagined myself homesteading on the property like they did on the TV show *Little House on the Prairie* (I watched that show religiously into my teens), but with a *much* nicer house and a lot more modern conveniences than they ever imagined. I thought I'd raise some animals (whatever that meant), grow some vegetables, bake some pies (not that I'd ever baked a pie in my life), and maybe I'd sweep the porch once in a while (because they always seemed to be sweeping the porch on those TV farms). I don't know exactly what I thought I was stepping into, but I do know it didn't include any thoughts about what life on a ranch *really* meant, and I certainly didn't consider myself to be *homesteading*.

To be fair, I'd done my share of outdoor activities like backpacking, camping, and sleeping outside on the ground when I was younger. I cooked over an open fire, washed my hair with a bucket of cold water from a creek, and fished for my dinner in a mountain lake. By the time I moved to CC Blue, however, I was *way* past the point in life where sleeping on the ground seemed at all enticing. My idea of being in the "wilderness" had become decidedly more princess-y.

What I *did* imagine life on the Ranch including was *creating a self-sufficient lifestyle.* I really wanted to grow our own food and learn how to preserve the excess for us to use throughout the year. There was something very hardy and independent about the idea of taking bounty from the earth and utilizing everything from it. I could see myself learning how to "put up" pickles and tomatoes and figuring out how to make jams. I would even allow myself to think about raising animals as a food source, but I expected any of the processed meat to come to me on a Styrofoam tray wrapped in cellophane, like it came from the local grocery store (such a city girl). And let's be clear: I wasn't expecting to *live off the land*, as my reliance on certain foods (chocolate and potato chips, for starters) would never be made from scratch by me—*ever*.

But this was not an outlook I had always embraced.

I planted my first little backyard garden when Ally and A.J. were young. I remember laying out the plot of land on the south side of our first house in Louisville. Brian dug up a patch of grass that was about sixteen feet by four, and the kids and I placed garden pavers around the border to keep the lawn from growing back into our future garden. We planted all kinds of seeds, including lettuce, beans, corn, and peas, along with a few tomato plants, into nice straight rows. The whole family took part in diligently watering and weeding that small garden over the course of the summer, and we were all excited when the sprouts began to appear and finally produce some of the most delicious vegetables we'd ever enjoyed.

I had never been exposed to growing vegetables before this. Gardening was not something my parents ever did when I was a kid, so the idea of growing our own food was something I was extremely proud of. I talked (OK, *maybe* bragged) about it with the rest of my family. They were *very* impressed and also intrigued, because *none of them* had grown up with any kind of gardening either (Jews didn't do a lot of gardening when we were growing up, especially when they lived in the suburbs).

One cousin, Carol, who lived in New York City at the time, was particularly fascinated by our garden. During one of our phone conversations, she asked what we would do if we ended up with too many peas or beans or tomatoes. (She didn't really get how small our garden was.) I decided to blow her mind by telling her we'd simply "can" anything we couldn't eat. Of course, I had never *canned* anything in my life.

"*Can?*" she asked. "What do you mean you'll *can* them?"

"You know," I said, "you preserve the vegetables in cans for future use."

In fact, I had no idea how to can vegetables and no intention of actually doing it. I was just messing with her. But she was *so* impressed and kept mentioning it every time we talked. I didn't know how to tell her I was kidding. So I kept up the ruse because I was in Colorado and she was in New York. She'd never know the difference.

Until later that summer, when she and her husband, David, decided to fly to Colorado to help my parents celebrate their anniversary. (Of all the luck! Why did my parents need a big anniversary celebration that year?) As happy as I was to get the chance to see them, I knew they'd want to see our garden and all of the "canning" we had done. And as predicted, on a call prior to their visit, Carol said, "I'm so excited to come see your gardening and canning prowess when we get to town!"

But there was no gardening and canning prowess. I was a complete canning fraud.

I knew I had to come up with something before they arrived. Since our garden was pretty well depleted by then, I didn't have a lot to work with. The day before their visit, I went to the grocery store and bought six cans each of Del Monte tomatoes, corn, peas, and beans. Early the next morning, I meticulously half-buried each of the cans in nice, neat rows in the garden, with the labels facing up to show the pictures of the vegetables inside. "There!" I thought. "I have canned vegetables from my garden."

When they arrived, Carol and David immediately asked to see the garden and all of my canned goods. I proudly walked them outside and with a grand sweep of my arm showed them the plot of dirt, with the half-buried cans lined up in their rows. I declared, "Here's the result of my canning."

They were confused, and I was amused. I said in an almost-exasperated tone, "What were you really expecting? I'm not a farmer. I don't know how to *can*, for God's sake."

Standing in that garden all those years ago, I couldn't imagine myself ever figuring out how, or even *wanting*, to can all of the food we do now. I was, after all, a nice Jewish suburban girl (and a bit of a brat) who had worked in traditional jobs with absolutely no experience or desire to live any type of self-sustaining life.

Fast-forward twenty years and here I was, living on the Ranch, finding myself *wanting* to live that life of canning vegetables from my garden (and other homesteading-*ish* kinds of things). But I had no idea if I had what it took to do it. Who did I think I was? I had no idea what I was doing. Did I really believe I could just *decide* to reinvent myself without any experience or knowledge of how to do any of this? To me, there was nothing natural about this new lifestyle, and it was overwhelming to imagine myself *starting over* to learn it all—and in my mid-50s to boot.

But I was selling myself short.

I had everything I had learned and experienced in my life (*sans* the half-planted cans of Del Monte vegetables), which I brought with me to the Ranch. I was discounting everything I had *already done* and assumed none of it could apply to this new life. But I had a wealth of knowledge and experience developed over those fifty years, providing me many of the qualities, skills, and strengths I would need to build this Nxt life. I didn't need to know *everything* there was to know about farming or ranching to start doing it. This wasn't about starting over; it was about starting with a foundation from a past life full of experience and learned skills. Everything from my organizational and business skills to my design, decorating, and entertaining skills. Not to mention my wonderful skills as a mom to children and pets.

Plus, Matthew and I could draw on all the qualities of who we were together to make it happen. We both had a lot of energy and a strong desire to make this ranch something special. We were both hard workers. We weren't afraid of getting our hands (too) dirty, and we knew when it made more sense to hire someone to get something done, rather than try to do it ourselves. (This saved our relationship more than once!) We also made a great team. If anyone could reinvent themselves based on who they had been, we could!

Life Builds upon Itself

When your Nxt is something you've never done before, it's easy to disregard everything you've done in the past because what's in front of you is so different. However, you get to take everything you've done in your past life with you and apply it to your Nxt. Yes, that's right. You get to use everything you've ever learned in the past and build upon it as you move into your Nxt.

In other words, all of your life comes with you.

Why do I mention this? Because I see it over and over again with my coaching clients—and I saw it in myself as I was beginning my new life on the Ranch. We forget that we get to bring our whole selves with us as we look to make a change in our lives. We think if we haven't done something before, we'll have to figure it out from scratch, but it's never from scratch. It's easy to think what you already know won't matter. It does. Sure, you'll have to figure out the nuts and bolts of how to do a new job, maybe learn new skills or gather new information, but you'll also have your past experience, your inherent strengths, and your pre-honed skills to help you figure it out along the way.

I know I did.

I had been a student who always loved figuring out how to apply new knowledge and information in a way that would fit my way of life. I especially liked trying out new ways to do things and making up ways that best served me. So I could not only learn how to do ranching and farming but figure out how to do it our way.

I had been a daughter, a wife, a mom, and an animal lover who loved being a caregiver to those who depended on me. Simply put, I had a nurturing personality—so it was natural for me to figure out how to raise farm animals once I knew the basics of caring for them.

I had been a camp director, party thrower, and conference creator. I knew how to bring people together for a great time. So establishing CC Blue as a destination for family, friends, and guests was much like figuring out how to host a bunch of people on the property—with the same level of attention to detail I had done so many times before.

You get to take everything you've done in your past life with you and apply it to your Nxt.

I had been a business owner, creator, and leader. I knew how to build and grow an organization and its people. Applying those skills to developing our own organization and the systems we needed to build our various lines of business would tap into all of that business acumen I had already developed. I would have been paralyzed from taking any Nxt steps if I hadn't been able to realize that I got to bring my whole life with me into this Nxt. I wasn't starting all over again. I was capitalizing on all that I had already learned and developed in my life.

All the steps you've taken throughout your life create a stronger and stronger foundation on which to build your next challenge. Of course, you also get to choose what you want to take with you and what you'd like to leave behind (hence the Del Monte canned vegetables don't appear in our garden today). So, if you've done work you've hated in the past, don't build that type of work into your Nxt. If you recognize there's a certain type of person you don't want to associate with anymore, please don't include that type of person in your Nxt.

Your Skills Come with You

Skill: The Ability to Do Something Well

Your skills form the foundation for *how* you will do your Nxt. They help you understand the ways you work best. Are you detail-oriented, or do you think of the big picture? Do you create plans, or are you better at following instructions? Do you like to work with your hands or put ideas on paper? Determining what skills you have and how best to apply them to a new situation is crucial to successfully navigating any change in your life.

I'm convinced *now* that each part of my life leading up to the Ranch had been building toward this Nxt stage. I just didn't know it earlier. I thought that because I had no prior experience, I had nothing to contribute, but when I stopped and listed some of the skills I already had, I realized there were lots of things I had developed in my "past" life that I could tap into as we were building CC Blue:

- ✧ I was a great organizer.

- ✧ I was a badass project manager.

- ✧ I liked to figure out *how* to do new things.

- ✧ I was good at designing different kinds of spaces.

I had the skills. Now I needed to figure out how to apply them to this new life.

Knowing that gardening and canning were important to creating our self-sustaining lifestyle, Matthew and I had to figure out how to make it happen. He had some gardening experience in various backyard gardens, but we were thinking our garden would be on a bigger scale. Not big in terms of farming lots of acres, but certainly bigger than anything either of us had tackled in the past. As we began talking it through, I realized it was just a big *project* requiring a healthy blend of organization, research, and design. We had to design the garden space, create a planting schedule, plan a rotational watering and weeding system, harvest the veggies as they were ready for picking, and, finally, learn how to preserve whatever was appropriate for canning or storing. All of it tapped into my badass project management, organizational, and design skills.

Canning was probably the biggest challenge we faced, as it was equal amounts art (what recipes to use), coupled with a healthy dose of "you better do it right or you could kill someone with botulism" science. Having no idea how to prepare anything for a can (pro tip—it's really a jar), we did some googling, bought some books about preserving, and started to collect all of the equipment necessary to begin the canning process. In no time, large canning pots and pressure cookers, jars of every size (with corresponding lids and bands), pickling mixes and lemon juice, pectin for jams, and vinegar by the gallon started to fill up our garage shelves.

After each harvest, we tried to preserve and can as much as possible. We soon learned the boiling times and cooking methods for different jams; preserves; tomato sauce; applesauce; sauerkraut; pickles; and vegetables like corn, beans, and peas. Our pantry shelves started filling up. We were eating the vegetables as we picked them from the garden, but we were also regaled with our prized possessions during the cold winter months. All of it was living up to my original romantic vision of living off the bounty of our land in a self-sustaining way.

Make a list of your skills. Not the things you do at work that are job-specific, but the skills underlying the job you do. Those skills are transferable. They come with you no matter what you end up doing in your Nxt.

Identify and Capitalize on Your Strengths

Strengths—Character Traits that Are Positive

As a leader within my company, I was a firm believer that we should identify our employees' strengths to make sure they were using those strengths to do their best work. Now, as a business coach, I believe everyone should begin their Nxt journey from a place of strength, focusing on what they do best. When working with my clients, I often ask them to take a strength assessment* so they can recognize what strengths they inherently have, in order to capitalize on them moving forward into their Nxt.

Starting from a place of strength is especially important when stepping into something new.

Starting from a place of strength is especially important when stepping into something new. Knowing whether you're a strong leader or a wonderful independent thinker; whether you thrive with data and information before deciding or you'd rather get input from others

---

*I have always used the Gallup Clifton StrengthFinders Assessment.

before taking action; whether you're a strategic thinker or more of a real-time doer (just to name a few strengths) will help you understand what you can leverage from within, and how you can thrive in a new situation.

When I took a good look at my strengths, I realized (and remembered):

⬧ I'm really good at visualizing the future and seeing the steps to get there.

⬧ I optimize everything I do.

⬧ I see the unique qualities in others, have an ability to communicate well, and am able to develop strong relationships.

By recognizing my strengths, I was able to use them and *apply them* to the very different life we were stepping into at the Ranch.

As someone who could visualize the future and see the steps to get there, I knew I could trust what I saw and create a plan. I was able to begin with the Main House and Guest House and then expand to the rest of the property, setting the location and purpose of each new structure along the way. From there I was able to plan how everything would *work together* to create the environment *and ambience* that would become CC Blue.

As an optimizer, I knew I would do everything it took to figure out how to set up the kind of lifestyle that would meet our needs. I realized the Guest House would be vacant a good part of the year, so I decided to maximize that space by doing short-term rentals to generate income, while also capitalizing on the farm animals and garden to enhance the experience of our rental guests.

Finally, as the infrastructure formed, I began to focus more on how I could weave *working* (the brainy kind—not the chores kind) into life on the Ranch. I yearned for more interaction with individuals and knew my years of business experience could help others. So I started my coaching business, working with individual clients from the Ranch (thank goodness for video conferencing) and then later moving to a unique coaching program *at* the Ranch.

As I look back on that first garden where I planted actual canned vegetables, I chuckle at the woman I was then and am just a bit surprised at the woman I've become today. My cousin sometimes reminds me of that earlier time, saying, "Look at you! Who would have ever believed you would be who you are today?" Luckily, I got to bring my life with me to help me along the way.

Important Takeaways

✧ You get to take everything you've done in your past life *with you* and apply it as you move into your Nxt.

✧ Your skills form the foundation for *how* you will do your Nxt.

✧ Make a list of your skills. All of them.

✧ Starting from a place of strength is *especially* important when stepping into your Nxt.

✧ Figure out what you might need to fill in with additional information, people, or other resources.

✧ Be intentional about what you choose and take along only those things from your life that will serve you best.

✧ Canning is a great way to preserve your harvest for future use. When in doubt, however, you can always plant a bunch of cans in your garden.

10

Figure It Out

CHAPTER 10

Figure It Out

Action and reaction, ebb and flow, trial and
error, change—this is the rhythm of living.

—BRUCE BARTON
Author, advertising executive, politician

The idea of homesteading expanded exponentially with the introduction of our first animals (chickens) onto the farm. We knew we wanted farm-fresh eggs as a part of our self-sustaining lifestyle, but neither of us had any experience in raising chickens. We had a ton of questions: How old should the chickens be when you get them? What do they eat? How much space do they need? Where do they sleep? How many eggs do they lay—and when? Pretty basic stuff, but we didn't know the answers to any of it, so we needed to learn a lot about how to keep these guys (or should I say *girls*) alive and content.

We brought in our first flock of chicks during the spring of the first year we were living full-time on the Ranch. We learned from our neighbors, who were raising about 300 chickens and selling their eggs to folks in the valley, that there were different breeds of chickens that laid different-colored eggs. *What? There are different-colored eggs that come out of chickens?* Well, I grabbed on to that piece of information like a dog with a bone and began researching which breed of chicken would lay blue eggs, because, *come on*, it seemed only right that any eggs coming from chickens at CC Blue should be *blue*.

The breed we settled on were called Araucanas. They looked like any ordinary chicken, with white, black, or gray feathers (which they call a "Blue Araucana," but it's not really blue, which was disappointing). We weren't able to find any locally, so I went online to see where in Colorado I could get them. Eventually I found a breeder (or hatchery, as they are often called) in the Midwest who specialized in Araucanas and other cool fowl. So we ordered a dozen baby chicks online. That's right. We ordered our baby chicks through a mail-order catalog. (*Head slap!*)

The website promised to ship their chicks the day they were born: "All baby chickens, ducks, geese, or turkeys will be shipped through the mail in secure boxes and guaranteed to arrive within 48 hours." OK. Apparently this was a common thing in farming, but still a bit shocking to me because shipping newborn animals through the mail wasn't really a thing in my nice, quiet suburban upbringing.

I don't know what I was expecting, but, as promised, a box arrived at our local post office two days after our chicks were born. I got a call early in the morning from the lady at the post office before it opened, telling me that our baby chicks had arrived and I should come right over to get them. It was 6:30, and Matthew and I threw on our coats and drove the three miles to the post office in record time. My baby chicks had arrived!

I ran to the back door of the post office as instructed and knocked loudly to let her know I was outside. She came to the door and handed me a small (10 x 6 x 6) brown box with holes poked in the top and the words "live animals" stamped on it. She told me to take care of those babies and get them into a heated space with some fresh water as soon as I could. She had obviously done this before and could probably see I had not. I certainly appreciated the advice and brought the box quickly into the heat of the car, where Matthew was waiting.

We eagerly opened the box to find some shredded paper, a small plastic cup of what I assumed *had been* water, and eleven two-day-old fluffy yellow chicks, chirping frantically. They huddled together in the center of the box, looking up at me eagerly with what I assumed was a desperate plea for food and water. I petted each of their tiny heads in reassurance and then saw the twelfth chick in the corner, lying all by herself, not making a sound, facing the wall of the box, and breathing heavily. I looked up at Matthew and said, "We need to get home—*now*." We didn't have anything with us to keep them warm or get them hydrated. I put the box inside my jacket to try to warm them, but instinctively I knew we had one chick in serious trouble. And if we didn't get the others some water and warmth as soon as possible, they'd all be in the same condition before we knew it.

We had done some research before the chicks arrived and learned that they needed to be in a very warm cage (a brooder), with a heat lamp to keep the interior at 95 degrees for the first week of their lives. Before their arrival, we had borrowed a small animal kennel, a heat lamp, and a chicken waterer from a friend and purchased some baby chick food from the local Murdoch's Ranch & Home Supply store. We had *just* enough information and supplies to get started, but the rest we'd have to experience and learn on our own.

> *Raising chickens took quite a bit of muss and fuss and ended up not being a frivolous thing at all.*

Luckily, I had thought to turn on the heat lamp in the brooder, which we were keeping in our kitchen, before we'd left for the post office. As soon as we pulled up to the house, I ran inside with the chicks and quickly placed the eleven chirping chicks in the kennel under the heat lamp and filled up their waterer and food tray. They stayed huddled together under the heat lamp for about ten minutes and then one by one each ventured over to the waterer to get their fill.

I sat on the floor next to the brooder, watching to make sure each one moved around, got water, and started to eat. Meanwhile, I held that twelfth chick in the palm of my hand, wrapped in a soft washcloth, trying to get her to take some water from an eyedropper. Matthew was googling how to care for a sick baby chick and reading instructions to me about stroking her throat to get her mouth to open and being sure to keep her warm. I thought we were making progress. She was so small (all two ounces of her) and so helpless, but I was totally convinced we could save her.

Then she suddenly died. In my hands.

I was like, "Noooooooo!" My heart sank. This was *not* supposed to happen. None of my baby animals were supposed to die.

To be honest, I hadn't given much thought to the idea that our chickens, or any of our animals, could die while living with us. I thought only about the upside of raising chickens: You get cute baby chicks. You raise them (which seemed like fun). Then you get cool, farm-fresh blue eggs from them. No muss, no fuss.

Which was actually not true. Raising chickens took quite a bit of muss and fuss and ended up not being a frivolous thing at all. Less than an hour after those first chicks arrived, I realized they depended on us for *their survival*. This was serious stuff. After that first baby chick died in my hands, I made it my mission to make sure those remaining eleven chicks stayed healthy, safe, *and* alive.

Thank goodness the chicks flourished over the next few months (or I would have been a wreck). I read everything I could about raising healthy chickens and took my job of being their foster chicken mom very seriously. As they grew out of their small kennel (which happened in no time), we moved them to a larger cage so they'd have more room to move around. I was also realizing these little birds were incredibly dirty creatures who were also starting to resemble baby velociraptors (the whole cute baby chick thing lasted a matter of days). Even with just eleven of them, they created a *ton* of dust from their tiny feathers, which traveled absolutely everywhere. I was more than ready to remove the ever-molting dinosaur birds as soon as possible from our kitchen into the generally dirtier surroundings of the garage, until it was warm enough to move them outside into their permanent home.

Oh right. Their permanent home. We still hadn't figured that one out yet.

Our neighbors had their 300 chickens living in an old barn on their property and let them run free during the day (free-ranging). This totally fit into my romantic notion of the ol' homestead, with chickens pecking on the grounds outside the house. In reality, however, skunks and foxes were picking off our neighbors' chickens one by one in record number, blowing that romantic vision all to hell. The idea of finding the remains of dead chickens in the yard was not what I had in mind. So we decided our chickens would not range freely, ensuring they would never be available to the death squad of predators roaming the area.

We found a big fancy chicken coop (a little chicken fortress) a few towns away. It could accommodate twelve chickens and came complete with a six-foot-long *enclosed* raised section with chicken wire all around it, which the chickens could access through a cute little chicken door from the interior sleeping roost. It had two sections of nesting boxes (for egg laying) and a storage area above for their feed. It even had a blue metal roof.

Once we moved our chicks into the fancy coop, they took to their new home in no time. To put them inside to sleep at night, one of us would get into the enclosed area with them and shoo them around until they ran up their ramp through the door into the roost. It was kind of chaotic, with a bunch of squawking and feathers flapping, but we'd eventually get them in and reward them with chicken feed before closing them in for the night. Soon, however, we observed that once they knew where they were supposed to sleep at night, they climbed up the ramp on their own and took their roosting spots as soon as the sun began to set. We didn't have to force them to do it. We didn't have to shoo them in. We just needed to show them where they would safely be spending the night, and they would go in on their own. Who knew?

Within a few weeks of living in the new coop, another chicken behavior started to emerge. We began to notice that some of our chickens were missing some of their tail feathers, which seemed odd. Fearing that some of our girls were getting sick, I googled "missing tail feathers" and discovered that hens will sometimes peck at each other (yep, that's where the term *hen-pecked* comes from) when they are bored and/or don't have access to foraging and pecking at the ground.

> *Trial and error forces us to understand what's wrong with our initial assumptions, what's missing from our information, and what we didn't know when we started out.*

We realized our chickens needed more space than our fancy fortress provided. As secure as it was, it wasn't big enough for the chickens to run around to do their *outside* chicken activities, like dirt bathing and ground scratching (which apparently is important for their health and sanity). So even though our chickens would not be free-ranging, they would still need a secure chicken yard so they could run around to do those important chicken things.

Which would require specific chicken fencing.

We ordered our first chicken fence online—for chicken "hobbyists." It turned out to be a cheap, flimsy mess. I don't know what we were thinking. We weren't hobbyists. We were serious chicken raisers. We knew as soon as we took it out of the box that it probably wouldn't hold up, but we put it up anyway. Every day we'd come outside to find the fencing lying down in one area or another, with our chickens taking advantage of the downed fence, running around *outside* the enclosed area, having flown the coop (yep, that's where *that* saying comes from), forcing us to spend what seemed like hours rounding them up. Luckily, we didn't lose any of our chickens with that first fence, but we knew we had to make a change.

Our second fence was much sturdier, more secure, and *electrified* with solar power (obviously for people serious about raising chickens). However, the battery system we installed to keep the wire "hot" was faulty (and cheap), and we found evidence of predators making their way into the chicken yard at night (but not into the fortress, so no chickens were lost—*thank goodness*).

On the third try, we figured out the most reliable battery to keep our fence electrified, keeping our chickens in and the predators out. At last I felt our chickens were safe and secure.

By late summer, we opened one of the nesting boxes and found our first tiny blue egg. While those first little eggs are edible (delicious, actually), they were also an important signal that our chickens had entered early adulthood and would soon grow into full-blown egg-laying hens in the weeks to come. It took six months and a lot of ups and downs, but we found ourselves with those farm-fresh eggs we had hoped for!

At first it seemed like an easy decision to bring chickens onto the property as our first farm animals, but it took a lot of trial and error to learn how to raise them. We had to think through what kind of chickens to get and then be prepared with the proper setup once they arrived. We had to be thoughtful about their shelter and safety and learn what they would need to thrive as they grew into adult chickens. We had to educate ourselves and accept responsibility for their well-being. By doing so, we finally received the benefit of having beautiful, healthy chickens with delicious blue farm-fresh eggs for ourselves.

More importantly, though, raising chickens was one of the first boxes we were able to check off as most important to us about living this lifestyle—becoming self-sustaining. Raising chickens was certainly not going to meet all our needs, but it was a first big step in taking on the responsibility of raising animals that would provide us with a food source.

We learned several lessons along the way, which would serve us as we continued to add new animals to the Ranch. They're also helpful lessons for anyone who's finding their Nxt.

Take Your Decisions Seriously

When that first baby chick died in the palm of my hand, I was affected deeply. From that moment, I felt a deep sense of responsibility for the ongoing care of all of the remaining chicks. We were their caretakers and needed to take our decision to raise them very seriously and make sure we protected them from harm. Their lives depended on us.

Even if your Nxt doesn't have the gravity of a little chick's life in the balance, the decisions at every step of the way should always be taken seriously. It could mean a major change in your life. It could affect your income, your relationship, or your way of living. There are always consequences for our behaviors and actions, and even if we are not solely responsible for each repercussion, we should act as if we are. Thoughtfulness and planning for each step as you move along your Nxt will help you address all of the needs and nuances in its development.

When I work with my coaching clients to help them in their search for what's Nxt, we move through a process of figuring out what's most important to them in order to take their decisions seriously. As I noted in Chapter 6, those criteria become the reason to say yes or no. And the clearer you are about the reason(s) you are deciding, the easier that decision becomes.

For us, the decision to raise chickens was clearly about beginning our self-sustaining lifestyle. Chickens would provide us eggs and set the stage for introducing additional farm animals to the property. But chickens also represented our stepping into the next stage of CC Blue. We were becoming a farm. We were raising animals. We were setting up the first of our branding opportunities:

blue eggs. We were starting to incorporate the *Big Why* of our next stage of living on the property and figuring out how to live it, day by day.

Embrace Trial and Error

Even with the best of intentions to do everything right the first time, we had no way around starting by trial and error. We didn't know enough through experience yet. We had to figure out what our baby chicks needed to survive, and then what was needed for our adult chickens to thrive. It took us three times to get the fencing to work around the chicken coop. Each time something failed, we redesigned and made the next iteration better. We didn't accept the failings of the first design and risk the well-being of our chickens. We continued to figure it out and eventually designed a system to make it work. It took us almost eight years and the installation of a permanent non-electrified fence to *finally* get a system that met our needs and those of our chickens.

Starting your Nxt journey may not work out as planned the first time, and that's OK. Trial and error forces us to understand what's wrong with our initial assumptions, what's missing from our information, and what we didn't know when we started out. The important thing is to adapt, adjust, and redesign plans to reflect your increased knowledge.

It's not uncommon for my coaching clients to come to the Ranch for an Immersion with a very succinct and well-laid-out plan, only to go through the process of finding their Nxt and realizing that their initial assumptions no longer make sense. Their original idea usually stays the course, but through our discussions and their own trial and error, they often adjust their thinking and adapt their plans based on their newfound information. That process continues as their idea turns into action, and their day-to-day experiences demand they refine and redesign their original idea again and again.

Trial and error are not to be avoided; they're to be embraced and learned from.

Learn from Your Mistakes

We didn't know enough when we first got those chicks to realize what we needed to learn. But with each step, and each mistake, we learned what they needed to eat, how they needed to sleep, and what kind of outside space they needed to thrive. Most important, perhaps, we learned how to keep those first chickens, and those that came after them, safe and alive.

Failure exists only when we don't learn from our mistakes. So, if we learn, then it's really trial and error. Which is a good thing.

In Chapter 3, I talked about the fears that block us from moving forward. One of the greatest fears many of us face is the Fear of Failure, and unfortunately, making mistakes is often equated with failing. But (again) failure exists only when we don't learn from our mistakes. So, if we learn, then it's really trial and error. Which is a good thing. We try, we learn, we adapt, we try again. We learn from our errors. We don't give up—we start another trial.

When finding your Nxt, learning from your mistakes is crucial to moving forward. There's no such thing as failure when moving into your Nxt, just gaining more information and insight, as long as you are willing to learn and adjust accordingly.

Our mistakes on the Ranch are almost too numerous to count. Not just with the chickens, but pretty much at every step of the way. We picked the wrong flooring in the house. We chose bamboo because it was a more sustainable wood—which checked off an important criterion for us—but with multiple dogs and Matthew in the house, it simply didn't hold up. We had to learn from that mistake and replace it (ten years later) with a hard oak floor that could withstand our demanding lifestyle.

We also made countless mistakes in the types of vegetables we planted in the garden, in the way we tried to move our cows from one place to another, and in the kind of plants we used for our landscaping. We learned and made changes. We adapted our behaviors and redesigned the way we did things. None of them was a failure in the end, because we always learned from our mistakes.

Important Takeaways

❖ Making decisions about moving into your Nxt should be taken seriously.

❖ You're always going to make mistakes. It's OK. It's part of the process of finding your Nxt.

❖ Trial and error are about adapting to what you learn: Adapt, adjust, and redesign.

❖ Trial and error are not to be avoided; they are to be learned from: We try, we learn, we adapt, and we try again.

❖ I'm repeating this because it needs to be repeated—failure exists only when we don't learn from our mistakes.

❖ If you buy chicks through the mail, be prepared with water and a warm blanket when you pick them up at the post office. They'll need both!

11

*Determine
Your Criteria*

CHAPTER 11

Determine Your Criteria

*Try to turn as many soft, aspirational goals
as possible into success criteria, and make
them specific enough that you can actually tell
whether or not you've met them.*

—ERIN KISSANE
The Elements of Content Strategy

Now that we had successfully incorporated chickens into our lifestyle, I turned my attention to adding more animals on the Ranch. There was a large herd of beautiful black-and-white cows on our neighbors' property, and I would watch them grazing from my office and be enamored by how they seemed to enhance the view. The cows had thick black curly coats and a large white band across their middle—kind of like an Oreo cookie. They were a Scottish breed called Belted Galloways—or "Belties," as they're known around here—and they were beautiful. They weren't an ordinary-looking cow (which I liked), more like a boutique breed, and I thought they'd make a perfect addition to CC Blue.

Of course, we knew nothing about raising cows, but, like everything else, we would figure it out.

Matthew and I approached Katie (that neighbor) to see if she would be willing to sell us some of her cows. That seemed the most obvious place to start.

"Sure," Katie said. "But I guess it depends on how many you want to start off with?"

I thought, *Is there a correct number of cows people usually start off with?*

"It also depends on what you plan to do with them," she continued.

Do with them?

It was becoming clearer and clearer to Katie that we were city folk.

Honestly, I hadn't thought about what we would *do* with them, other than have them look pretty in our pasture. But Matthew was a lot more pragmatic. He knew they were meat cows, so he assumed we'd raise them for their beef. We were, after all, looking for ways to produce our own food. Other than knowing that beef came from cows, we had no practical knowledge about what that would mean in terms of raising them for their meat.

We told her we'd probably want to raise some for meat and just have some (looking pretty) on the property.

"So probably a mix of heifers and steers?" she asked.

We looked at each other with that "We have no idea" kind of look and responded with, "What would *you* suggest?"

It was becoming clearer and clearer to Katie that we were city folk.

Luckily, Katie was a kind woman who was willing to take the time to explain some of the basics of raising cows. She told us a heifer was a young female who hadn't yet had a calf, and a steer was a male that had been castrated. Then she asked us a series of questions, which, at first, made our heads spin, but ultimately helped us think through the idea of raising cows in more detail.

- ⋄ "Are you interested in building a herd by breeding them?"

- ⋄ "If you want to raise them for beef, are you looking to keep the beef for yourself or would you be looking to sell it?"

- ⋄ "Have you thought about how much hay you can either grow or buy to support your herd, and how you'll provide water for them?"

- ⋄ And finally: "Have you checked your fences to make sure they're strong enough to keep your cows in the pasture?"

Oh—my—God.

It was clear we hadn't thought through any of those things, so there was no way we could answer any of these questions.

She was asking us to define our criteria for bringing cows into our care, and we hadn't given any thought to it except for "Maybe it would be cool to have some cows in our pasture."

I was totally embarrassed. I knew better than to frivolously step into a decision like this. This was a big deal, and we needed to take it much more seriously.

Katie, being a seasoned rancher, suggested we do some research to answer all of her earlier questions and to determine:

1. Were Belties the type of cow we wanted to raise (since there were many breeds we could choose from)?

2. And, assuming they were, how would we set up our pastures to take care of them (or whatever kind of cow we chose instead)?

If, after doing the research, we still wanted to purchase her cows, she said she would be willing to sell us a small herd to get us going.

Over the next few weeks, we buckled down and did our homework. We reviewed all of Katie's questions and determined the main criteria we needed to raise cows safely at the Ranch. We learned:

1. We needed to make sure our perimeter fences were secure, because cows tend to walk around their boundaries each day, looking for any weak spots to escape. We also learned that if we didn't want the cows grazing around the house (which we decidedly did not), we'd need to put up an interior boundary fence between the house and the pasture to keep them off the lawn.

2. We also needed a trough for water, in a spot the cows could easily access and we could easily refill daily.

3. Finally, we needed to either grow and/or purchase enough hay to feed them through the winter.

Once we were relatively sure we had checked off the necessary preliminary boxes, we approached Katie to buy some cows. She had a pair of older female cows who had each given birth to a calf in the past six months (one heifer and one steer), which we all agreed would give us a great start. We'd have four cows, two of which were more settled and mature, and two babies, which would make me very happy.

The next day, Katie brought the two mama cows with their babies to our property and released them into our pasture. As if on cue, the two pairs began walking the fence lines to check out their boundary and scope out any weaknesses. To our delight, they didn't find any.

Until about three days later.

That's when the cows discovered that one section of our temporary interior fence had fallen down. They were able to walk right over the downed wire. Soon after that, we found them grazing on the newly sodded lawn in front of our house. Luckily, our friends Lindsay and Jason were visiting at the time, and we were able to enlist their help to "round up" the cows and return them to the pasture. Our friends were thrilled! It seemed like a simple enough thing to do and very *ranchy* as well.

Of course, none of us had any idea what to do, so we instinctively ran outside waving our arms around, shouting some version of "Heeya!" and "Yeehaa!" at the top of our lungs, all in an effort to get the cows to move from the lawn to the pasture, where they belonged.

The yelling and the arm waving got them moving, but instead of getting them to the pasture, they spooked and took off in a full run down our driveway, toward the road. Without giving it a second thought, all four of us ran after them, still yelling ridiculously and waving our arms—trying desperately to catch up to them to stop them from reaching the county road.

Somehow, Matthew and Jason got in front of the cows and were able to stop them from running into traffic (not that we had much traffic) and miraculously turned them back toward the driveway.

Lindsay and I then stationed ourselves at the bottom of the driveway as a human barrier to stop the cows from continuing down the road in the other direction from our property (which, can I say, was one of the scariest things I've ever done, with four cows running directly toward us). Luckily (thank God!), the cows made the wise decision to turn up the driveway at the sight of us standing there with terrified looks on our faces. They ran past the new lawn and back into the pasture.

There was a huge collective sigh as the four of us—panting heavily—made our way back up the driveway and out toward the pasture to fix the fence. As we got to the downed fence, however, we saw that two of the cows weren't going back through the opening into the pasture. They were just standing there, not trusting the downed wire to walk back over it, as if they had forgotten that was the way they'd escaped the pasture in the first place.

So the guys began running toward them *again* to encourage them go through the opening. Instead (as we should have expected), the pair turned and bolted back toward the house. As soon as *those two* started running away from the pasture, the other two went through the opening (no trust issues on their part) and ran straight toward their friends.

Now the cows were running in a big circle from the lawn to the pasture, jumping over and breaking another part of the fence, then back to the lawn and around to the pasture again. Around and around they went. We just kept running after them, waving and shouting.

We stopped chasing them, and they stopped running.

This went on for about six or seven rounds before we got so tired we couldn't yell or wave our arms anymore. We all stood in various locations around the lawn or the pasture with our hands on our knees, panting. The cows, who were on their last circle back toward the downed part of the fence, crossed easily back over the wire, walked to the middle of the pasture, and settled down to eat.

We stopped chasing them, and they stopped running.

Just. Like. That.

We all looked at each other and realized *we* had been causing the cows to run. (*Collective head slap!*)

Not wanting to repeat this scenario again, Lindsay positioned herself at one of the downed sections of the fence, and I positioned myself at the other. Matthew and Jason went for supplies, and within thirty minutes the interior fencing was back in place. All was good with the world again. Just to play it safe, we walked the entire perimeter of the pasture fence to make sure there were no weak spots. Once satisfied that no more escapes were imminent, we returned to the house to sit on the somewhat trampled new lawn and drink some much-deserved adult beverages—even though it was only nine in the morning.

Luckily, no cows (or friends) were injured (only our pride) during that whole debacle, but we certainly learned two important lessons that day:

1. Chasing animals will only get them to run away—and in the opposite direction from where you want them to go.

2. We would need a much better fencing plan if we wanted to keep animals on the property.

I sure hoped Katie wasn't home that morning watching us. If she was, I'm sure she just shook her head and said, "City folk."

Each Next Step

Sometimes when we think about what's Nxt, we assume it will be *one* thing. One change. One decision. Or one *next* step (the smaller ones) to get there. In reality, sometimes there can be multiple *next* steps to finding, and *achieving*, your Nxt.

I don't tell you this to scare you off; I tell you this so you'll be prepared for the *process* of finding your Nxt.

Changing a job can seem like one step, but there are many considerations that go into the final decision to choose one job over another. The process can entail many steps. The same holds true for making a change in a relationship. On the surface, it may appear that the next iteration with your partner will require a small tweak or adaptation of behavior, but then, as you dig deeper, you find that multiple changes are required to step into what is Nxt for both of you.

Luckily, the process for each next step is repeatable. You don't have to start from scratch each time; you should recognize the patterns to follow and consider them at each step of the way. As we discussed in earlier chapters, each next step begins with

1. determining an overarching theme about where you want to go Nxt (seeing),

2. making a list of what's most important to you, and

3. using those to help make decisions that will serve you.

I now want to add two more concepts: Determining the Criteria *for* your actions and Defining the Benefits *of* those actions.

Determining Your Criteria

Criteria: a principle or standard by which
something may be judged or decided.

Once you have an overarching theme for what you are trying to accomplish, determining the criteria for each step of your Nxt creates the context for you to work within and allows you to narrow down the specific actions needed to make it happen.

Determining your criteria *before* you take any action helps you define specific tasks necessary to achieve your goals. These tasks might include a list of work requirements, people requirements, or even value requirements. Simply put, the criteria you set up will give you clarity about the nitty-gritty stuff that will have to get done to make your Nxt step happen.

My coaching clients often worry that finding their Nxt will be focused *only* on big-picture thinking, but they quickly realize there's no way to make their Nxt *happen* without getting clear about:

1. What they want to accomplish,

2. the criteria for their actions at each step
    of their Nxt, and

3. the specific tasks required for success.

For us, the creation of our lifestyle at CC Blue was composed of a series of next steps over the course of years, causing us to treat each one as its own little Nxt. In essence, the Ranch was evolving from one Nxt to the Nxt.

For this Nxt in the evolution of CC Blue, our overarching theme was *raising cows*.

The first criterion we determined to do that effectively was to set up a safe and proper environment for our cows *before* purchasing them and bringing them on-site. This gave us clarity about the specific tasks required to bring cows on the property. We could then make a list of what we needed to do to accomplish our goal of getting cows.

The most immediate tasks we needed to accomplish included:

- ✓ Checking our existing perimeter fence to make sure it was secure and setting up an interior fenced area to keep the cows in the pasture and off our lawn.

- ✓ Provide easy access to water for the cows and easy access for us to refill the water daily.

- ✓ Determine how much hay our cows would require over the winter months and purchase enough until we could figure out how to grow and "put up" hay from our own pasture.

By understanding the specifics of what was necessary to bring cows to CC Blue, we were clear about the tasks we needed to complete before they arrived. In general, we were successful in setting up a safe and proper environment for our cows. Sure, we had an enormous amount to learn about animal management in general and a whole lot of fencing projects ahead of us (more next steps), but as we continued to build and develop CC Blue, we knew we'd serve ourselves best if we determined the criteria for our actions before we moved forward.

Understanding the Benefits

Benefit: an advantage or profit
gained from something.

The full context of gaining clarity about your Nxt can be achieved only by understanding the benefits behind your actions. Why bother doing all of this if it doesn't benefit you in some way—*right?*

Identifying *all* of the benefits your Nxt step will provide helps make sure you continue to relate your decisions to what is most important to you. It can be easy to get caught up in the more tactical exercises of setting up the criteria for your actions and forget to identify and acknowledge the benefits of doing so. Keeping the benefits front and center in your mind will provide the bigger context of the *Big Why* behind moving into your Nxt.

As we were deciding to bring cows onto the property, we asked ourselves why we really wanted them and how they would add to our evolving lifestyle. The answers were enlightening and helped tie our decision to what was really important to us.

1. As we were researching, we learned that having cows graze on our pastures would help to naturally keep the ground fertilized and the grass healthier, if we practiced good grazing techniques. This reflected our desire to be good stewards of our land and help make our pastures self-sustaining over time.

2. We wanted to raise our own cows as a source of clean beef—grass-fed and free from antibiotics and fillers. This supported our desire for growing our own food, and in turn, would help make us more self-sufficient.

3. We learned that Belted Galloways were really good for breeding (i.e., the mamas typically have easy calving and care for their young very well), allowing us to grow our herd in a natural way with relatively little drama. This further increased our self-sufficiency, as we'd be able to experience having babies!

4. We knew having cows would add to our lifestyle of being on a ranch and would add to the special nature of our farm and the whole ecosystem we wanted to create. Plus, we thought it would be very cool for our guests to be introduced to this special breed of cow.

Having a contextual picture of the benefits that each next step will provide you is so important to moving you fully into your Nxt—whether it includes cows or not.

Important Takeaways

❖ Finding Your Nxt will most certainly take many *next* steps (the smaller ones).

❖ You don't have to start from scratch each time, but you should define the criteria you want to follow and consider them during each next step along the way.

❖ Determining your criteria *before* you take any action helps you define specific tasks necessary to achieve your goals.

❖ Understand the benefits behind your actions. Why bother doing all of this if it doesn't benefit you in some way—*right?*

❖ Don't chase cows. They will always run in the opposite direction from where you want them to go.

12

Make It Up

CHAPTER 12

Make It Up

The problem is not making up the steps
but deciding which ones to keep.

—MIKHAIL BARYSHNIKOV
Dancer, choreographer, actor

After we felt like we had a handle on raising chickens and cows, our dream of raising more farm animals started to become a more frequent topic of conversation. It may not make sense, but the idea of adding more animals into our lives felt like an even bigger decision than pulling the trigger to move to the Ranch in the first place. It was a lot more responsibility, and I was hung up on the idea that there was a particular way we were supposed to do it.

We lived in a valley that was thought of as cattle country. Some folks had horses, and one of our neighbors had chickens, but it was really all about raising beef around here. We didn't know anyone else in the area with a full range of farm animals on their property. So it was easy to start thinking that raising cattle and a few chickens was the only way things were supposed to be done.

But we wanted to do it differently.

The challenge was, as much as I wanted to make up the way we wanted to do it, we were dealing with real live animals. I was worried there was some magic formula we needed to follow for running a farm in a particular way, with a particular number and configuration of animals. I figured there had to be a blueprint, or at the very least, rules about doing the whole farm animal thing, right?

Well, there wasn't.

Once I realized it was up to us to figure things out, my entrepreneurial creative juices kicked into high gear, and I was off and running.

There were certainly countless resources available about caring for different animals—and hundreds of actual blueprints for building a barn, but we needed to figure out how to design our entire farm at CC Blue. Truth be told, once I realized it was up to us to figure things out, my entrepreneurial creative juices kicked into high gear, and I was off and running.

I loved making shit up!

Our first step was to identify which animals and how many of each we wanted to raise. I made a rule early on that we'd never have fewer than two animals of any given species. From the little I knew about farm animals, they do best with companions or in a herd, so that became one of our operating principles from day one.

In terms of which animals, it came down to two factors:

1. They had to be a smaller breed (which we believed would be manageable for us as novice farm animal caretakers).

2. They had to be cute.

For me, the cuteness factor was *far more* important in choosing our species than it was to Matthew (shocking, I'm sure). But we were able to agree that a healthy mix of cuteness and manageability fit nicely into our personalities and lifestyle.

That's when I came up with the idea of raising miniature—or at least the smaller-sized—breeds of different species. I've always loved horses and felt a strong affinity toward them, but I was terribly intimidated by their size and strength and had little desire to ride them (couldn't quite get over the intimidation factor). So the idea of bringing miniature horses onto the property was a perfect compromise. And talk about raising the cuteness factor of the Ranch!

Next came the goats. Boy, do you hear horrible stories about goats. They eat tires. Destroy cars. They're supposedly smelly, aggressive, and difficult to handle. I don't know why I thought they'd be a great addition to our barnyard, but I had a gut feeling they'd be a perfect fit for us. Not the kind that eat tires or destroy cars, but the smaller-sized Pygmy and Nigerian Dwarf goats, which had a much nicer reputation and were also super cute.

To round out the mix, we decided to raise pigs. The obvious rationale for this was for their food contribution, but I also hoped they would add some cuteness as well. We found the perfect combination from a friend who was raising a small heritage breed of pig called Kunekunes (originally from New Zealand, which translates to "fat-fat" in Māori). They're slow-growing pigs who stay on the smaller side, are known to be extremely friendly and social, and produce wonderful pork and fat if we wanted to process them. And as pigs go, they're pretty damn cute.

Given that we were focused on raising smaller breeds, we recognized their shelter would have to be sturdy enough to provide safety from the mountain lions, bears, coyotes, foxes, and badgers that frequently roamed our area. Clearly, a barn designed to keep them enclosed at night was in order.

We had never designed a barn before, so *naturally* I went to Pinterest to get some ideas. As expected, there were a wide variety of barns on Pinterest. I didn't need a fancy barn, but I did want a nice barn—a workable barn. A barn that Matthew and I would want to spend time in and would serve the needs of our animals. To supplement Pinterest, we thought it prudent to talk with some local ranchers who had barns on their property.

Unsurprisingly, most thought we were nuts when we told them we were thinking about raising miniature animals. Their consistent reaction was, "What's the point?" They raised animals strictly for practical purposes. You ride horses to round up your cattle. You raise cattle for beef. You raise pigs for pork. And goats! Well, you're just crazy to raise them at all; this is cattle country. But they did give us great insights.

One guy told us a good barn had three things going for it: 1) fresh air moving throughout, 2) lots of natural light, and 3) a wide center aisle going through the whole barn.

Another told us we should include storage for feed and supplies and, if possible, give our animals direct access to an outside corral or pasture. The other criteria *we added* included a bathroom (it was a bit of a walk back to the house, after all), hot and cold running water (hindsight showed us this was the most brilliant thing we did), a broom closet, a feed and tack room, and an upstairs loft for storage (not hay storage—"stuff" storage). We now had a really good idea of what we needed.

Next we reached out to Jeff, the architect who had designed the houses on the property. We asked, "Want to design a barn for us?" He laughed at first and then realized we were serious (he has since learned if I call asking a "Would you want to . . ." question, I'm not kidding). Even though he had never designed a barn before, he agreed, without question, to take on the project.

> *We had never designed a barn before, so naturally I went to Pinterest to get some ideas.*

Within a few months of reaching out to Jeff, we had a blueprint for a barn in our hands, had created a fully thought-out budget, and had made the final decision to go ahead and make it happen. We were going to build a barn and bring mini horses, goats, and pigs to CC Blue! Nine months later, the barn was built, and we were ready to bring our animals to the Ranch.

The first to arrive were two goats, Rebel and Bella, and two mini donkeys, Megan and Sully. (I found them on Craigslist.) The goats were living with a woman who had them as companions for an older horse who had recently died. The donkeys were living on a property with lots of different animals, but there wasn't adequate space for them (they were living in a horse trailer). Obviously, they all needed to come to CC Blue.

The thing about finding animals on Craigslist, however, is you have to be willing to act, and act fast, if you want to get them. As willing as we were to do that, we didn't have any way to get them from the Denver area, six hours away, to the Ranch. We needed a trailer. Thanks to Craigslist (again), we found a small horse trailer for sale. We met the owners in the parking lot of our local Walmart, did the transaction, hooked up the trailer to our pickup, and drove over the mountains to get the goats at one stop and the mini donkeys at the second. Then we drove them back over the mountain to their new home at CC Blue. Luckily, I was able to find our mini horses at a farm less than two hours away, and now that we had the small horse trailer, drove there a couple of weeks after the goats and donkeys arrived. I loaded up the four minis and brought them back to the Ranch.

Now all we needed were the pigs.

The pigs I found were eight-week-old piglets, located (again) six hours away, but luckily they didn't require the horse trailer to transport them to the Ranch. Instead, I got out the animal crate we'd used for our baby chicks, lined it with blankets and towels, and brought it with me to pick up our pair of pigs. Ally had gone with me to pick out the piglets from a litter of about twenty, and, as we got them into the crate, she named one Rosie, and I named the other Olive. They were so dang cute!

And they were squealing like crazy.

She looked at me with that "Are you sure you want to do this?" look. Somehow, without hesitation, I got into the car with those two cute, squealing piglets (who were in their crate on the passenger seat next to me) and began the six-hour drive back to the Ranch. It was kind of insane, but at the same time, it seemed like the natural thing to do. I wasn't going to put them in the back of our truck. Or even in the back seat of the car. They were scared and confused. So, before reaching the highway, I turned the crate around on the seat so I could open its door and put my hand on the blanket between both of them to offer them some comfort and, hopefully, calm their fears.

It worked for a few miles. Then the squealing resumed.

I didn't know what to do, and I didn't want to endure the high-pitched squealing for the whole ride home, so I did what I used to do for my kids when they were babies and upset: I started to hum. I wouldn't torture my kids with my singing, but I could hum, so I used to hum lullabies (or an approximation of a lullaby) to them, and they'd usually fall asleep.

So I thought, *Why not?* I began humming to Rosie and Olive.

Within seconds they stopped squealing. Within a few minutes, they settled down into the blankets and closed their eyes. (I swear!) I couldn't believe it worked. I continued humming for the next few minutes. When I thought they were asleep, I stopped humming. Rosie immediately jumped up and started squealing again. *Damn it.* I started humming again, and she settled down.

I hummed for the next three hours. I could barely speak when I stopped for gas.

The next half of the trip started off with the girls squealing again and me settling them down by humming. Then Rosie sat up on her haunches and threw up all over the inside of the crate, her sister, Olive, and the car's front seat. Who the hell knew a pig could get carsick!

I parked on the side of the road, removed the crate, and placed Rosie and Olive in the back seat—where I tried to wash them off with a pack of baby wipes I had instinctively thrown into the car before leaving home. I took the soiled towels out of the crate and put them in the trunk, rearranged the clean towels and blankets in the crate, returned my two wiggling, squealing piglets to the crate in the front seat again, and resumed the drive—humming all the way home.

I can't believe I did it.

I can't believe we did all of it. We had a barn. We had animals. And we'd pretty much made up every aspect of this part of CC Blue. As many steps as it took us to get there, it was starting to feel like we were finally beginning to live out our dream.

Making It Up Requires a Different Perspective

Sometimes we need to release ourselves from the belief that there is only one way to do things. Further, we don't need to be locked into the way something is *supposed* to be done just because someone has done it a certain way before us. The idea of *making it up* is a way of challenging yourself to think differently about how to look at a problem or an opportunity. Instead of assuming there is a required way to get a problem solved, you can ask yourself, *How would I do it to best meet my needs*? Don't worry about how it's been done by others. You might find that you can make it up in a different way than it's ever been done before—one that serves you far better than you ever thought possible.

When we were looking to bring more farm animals on-site and design a barn for CC Blue, I initially thought there was one tried-and-true way of doing it. One set of rules. One magic formula for the type and number of animals you should have on a farm. But that was a narrow-minded approach. It held me back and limited my vision of what we *could* do. There was no master blueprint that every other property followed. We could make up every aspect about this place and design it all to meet our needs. We didn't have to replicate what other farmers had done before, unless we wanted to *learn* from them and *incorporate* their ideas into our plans.

When you allow yourself to make it up, you can tap into your creativity and imagine how things *could* be. You can take the best of what you know to be true and adapt it to meet your needs and serve your purpose. It is a change of perspective from *"How am I supposed to do it, based on how it's always been done?"* to *"If I could make it up to work for me, how would I do it?"*

It's an incredibly freeing way to look at your life—and your Nxt.

We've Always Done It That Way

When I was leading my company, I would sometimes be approached by an employee who was having a problem with one task or another in their job. After they explained the difficulty in completing the task, I would often ask, "Why do we do it that way?" If the employee answered, "Because we've always done it that way," the hairs on the back of my neck would stand up. I would look at them and say, "Well, if it's not working, how about we figure out a *new* way of doing it that will actually solve the problem?" In other words, we don't have to live with something that isn't working; we can make up a new way of doing it.

I've had many coaching clients who have felt stuck because they're in a loop of feeling like *the way they've always done something is the way it has to be done,* simply because they've always done it that way. Their perspective about the problem generally starts from a place of *what it is,* instead of *what could be.* When I ask them to tell me what their *ideal situation* would look like if they could have it meet their needs, they can usually point to one or two changes that would make things better, and they're shocked. They didn't think they could do it differently. They've been locked into a belief that, because they've always done something one way, it was the only way it could be done.

> *We don't have to live with something that isn't working; we can make up a new way of doing it.*

Another way to break the feeling that there is only one way to do things is to ask yourself, "How would I do it if I could start over, knowing what I know now?" The idea of being able to start over releases your mind from the walls it sets up to stop you from seeing other possibilities. It allows you to think about what *could* work and what you would change *knowing what you know now*. It gives you permission to release yourself from the restraints of how you think you're supposed to do something. It opens you up to thinking about how you could do it in a way that serves you best.

Intention Versus Momentum
(Again, Because It's That Important)

Deciding to act means you are moving forward with intention, not momentum. Decisions are powerful. They put a stake in the ground that signals the end of the initial phase of exploration of an idea and declares you have determined to *do* something. It doesn't necessarily mean you have all of the details worked out, but it does mean you have gathered enough information to make a plan to guide your actions—intentionally.

Momentum tends to take hold of the change process once we get the ball rolling. The excitement that comes from seeing the possibilities ahead can get you moving with an energy all its own. Allowing your actions to be driven by momentum *alone* means you are allowing the forces of energy and excitement to move you forward, without consciously *choosing* to move in that direction. It's like allowing the current of a stream to move you aimlessly along without using your own paddle to define the route you want to take. If you find yourself in this position, slow down. Ask yourself if you are *deciding* to move forward, or moving forward because momentum is taking you there.

As Matthew and I talked more and more about getting farm animals and building a barn, I'd get totally wrapped up in the excitement of the idea and swept up in the possibilities of it all. Which was great and exciting. But it was also a really big deal for us to move into this Nxt phase of the Ranch. It was a big investment. It was going to be a big change to our lifestyle. And it was going to take a lot of our time and energy to care for these animals. So I had to slow down and become crystal clear about how to proceed. We needed to be absolutely intentional about our actions—we couldn't afford for momentum to take us down this road without our choosing it. We had to make conscious decisions to ensure it would work for us.

And so we did.

Important Takeaways

⬧ Sometimes we need to release ourselves from the belief that there is only one way to do things.

⬧ The idea of *making it up* is a way of challenging yourself to think differently about how to look at a problem or an opportunity.

⬧ When you allow yourself to make it up, you can tap into your creativity and imagine how things *could* be.

⬧ If you ask why something is being done a certain way, and the answer is "Because we've always done it that way," the hairs on the back of your neck should go up.

⬧ Always ask yourself what you would change *knowing what you know now.*

⬧ Decisions are powerful. They put a stake in the ground that signals the end of the initial phase of exploration of an idea and declares that you have committed to *do* something.

⬧ Momentum tends to take hold of the change process once we get the ball rolling. Don't let momentum take you along without consciously *choosing* to move in that direction.

⬧ Contrary to popular belief, pigs can get carsick on a long drive. Be prepared.

13

Step into Your Nxt

CHAPTER 13

Step into Your Nxt

Hard things take time to do.
Impossible things take a little longer.

—PERCY CERUTTY
Coach of world-class runners

N ot long after the barn was full of animals and we felt pretty darn settled into this new life we were living, I decided it was time to step it up even more by birthing some animal babies on the Ranch. A voice inside me kept saying that until we bred our own animals, we weren't real ranchers. And I wanted to be a real ranch girl. Matthew was much more secure in his identity as a rancher at this point, but I wasn't feeling like I had earned the title yet. Even though I did chores, bucked hay, and cared for our animals alongside Matthew, I still felt like I was playing the role of a ranch girl rather than actually being one.

It's not as if we hadn't raised any babies on the Ranch. We had gained some experience when we purchased some of our goats, pigs, and chickens as newborns or at eight weeks old, but we hadn't experienced the birthing of any babies on-site. And that seemed like an important thing to do if we really wanted to step into this Nxt stage of life on the Ranch.

So, after some discussion, we decided to begin with breeding our goats, because I knew baby goats would instantly increase the cuteness quotient on the Ranch tenfold, and you now know that always factored into my decision-making with our animals. Seriously, goat kids are the epitome of adorable, so who wouldn't want to start with baby goats?

There were four female goats in our herd—Bella, Coco, Gaby, and Lily—each at a prime age for getting pregnant, except for Bella, who was a few years older than the other three and was also a different breed. She was a Pygmy goat, and the other three were Nigerian Dwarfs, so I wasn't sure if we could breed all the girls with only one male. A Pygmy goat's shape is very different (short and squat) and much smaller than a Nigerian Dwarf (who are leaner and a bit taller), but we read that interbreeding within the smaller goat breeds was a common practice, so we decided to move ahead to find one buck for all four of our girls.

The question was, "Where does one go to find a buck for this purpose?" I asked other goat owners in the area and got an unexpected yet consistent answer: "Check out Craigslist." I thought they must be kidding (pun intended). But I swear, people with "intact" male goats (as some refer to their bucks online) post their availability on Craigslist for the purpose of finding people like us to borrow their buck for a small stud fee. I couldn't believe it. But it made total sense, and it also made the process of finding a buck straightforward.

I found a two-year-old Nigerian Dwarf buck on Craigslist whose owner was more than happy to let him spend a couple of months at CC Blue to knock up our females (my term, not theirs). She wanted $10 per female (so $40 total) and assurances from us that we'd provide safe housing and appropriate feed during his stay. Done.

A week later, he arrived. I didn't know what to expect. I hadn't asked for a picture or description or anything really (total novice move), but I was immediately smitten as he jumped out of the back of the pickup and swaggered into our barn. He was very handsome (and he knew it), with his mostly white coat and beautiful striping of brown and black along his back and down his legs. He also had a decent set of horns, which made him look quite big. As we watched him enter the goat stall and adjacent fenced-in yard, he moved confidently from one girl to the other, checking each one out while (I suppose) assessing the prospect of their readiness. This boy was ready and willing to do the work he was brought here to do.[*]

Before his owner left, I asked about his name, only to learn he didn't have one. This was unacceptable to me, so I named him William. It fit him perfectly, even if it was (most likely) a temporary moniker.

William settled into his role within the herd quickly and with little drama. He was a delight to have around. He was kind of silly, loved to be scratched behind the ears and horns, and was the

---

[*] None of our goats had horns, so I was a bit nervous to see how and when he might use them in his interactions with our girls, as well as our two boys in the herd. But luckily, he never used them aggressively.

center of much flirtation from the girls as each one went into her cycle. It took only about six weeks before William's job appeared to be complete and it was time for him to go home. I was sad to see him go, but the prospect of having a breeding machine like him around all the time made us realize it was his time to go.

It was the best $40 we ever spent!

With this first task completed, it was time to learn all about, and prepare for, the birthing of our baby goats. I read everything I could get my hands on about goat birthing. I learned what signs would determine when they were close to labor, the position the kids should be in the belly, and all the problems that could go wrong with the births. Breech kids. Upside-down kids. Tangled twins unable to make it down the birth canal. Hoofs in the wrong places. Heads in the wrong places. And (no kidding!) it scared the heck out of me. But I thought, *Well . . . it's kind of late to go back now,* and I somehow knew we'd handle anything that came our way when the time for birthing arrived.

I hoped.

That's when I realized we didn't have a clue when that time would be. I kind of knew when they had conceived, but I had only a vague idea of the timing (like sometime during the month of January). I wasn't able to pinpoint an exact date for any of them.

Here's the thing: The gestational period for goats is 150 to 155 days after they conceive, so I really needed to know when they had conceived in order to do the math. And I couldn't do that.

So I made a whole lot of guesses, and as it turned out, I was absolutely terrible at predicting anything.

I picked an arbitrary (and very early) date during William's stay to start the 150-day clock running, and, because I was so excited and determined to be there when the birthing happened, I became obsessed about watching for any changes that might indicate impending birth for the better part of a month before any of the kids began to pop.

I'd spend day after day assessing the elasticity of each mama's rear haunches (as if I knew what I was trying to feel for), checking to see if any of their bellies had dropped, or looking for any discharge emerging from God-knows-where weeks before they ended up being due. I even went into the stall late one night and sat there for hours, totally convinced Lily was going to drop her baby any minute, only to leave after she lay down and gave me a side-eyed glare, daring me to stay a minute longer.

But then the babies finally started to come.

Coco was the first to go into labor. I noticed her standing in the stall first thing in the morning with her head pressed into the wall (a common behavior of early labor). Upon closer inspection, I saw that she was having contractions. I cleared the other goats out, moved her into an enclosed area we had set up for our mamas, and let her do her thing while I stood by to assist in any way she needed.

It was extraordinary.

She lay down in the hay and, with several pushes, got her baby out. She stood up almost immediately and began cleaning him off, and then suddenly lay back down again and pushed out another one! This time when she stood up, she ignored the second baby and went back to finish cleaning off her first. I realized I could help and picked up the second baby and wiped him off, clearing out his mouth and nose. I rubbed his chest and legs vigorously to get him to take some good deep breaths (having no idea how the heck I knew to do that). In less than a minute, he inhaled and let out a beautiful *baaaaah*, and after a quick snuggle, I put him near Coco to finish the job of cleaning him so she could get that sweet connection with both of her babies.

For the next week, we had babies every three days. Lily was next with a set of twin girls, then Gaby with her boy and girl. So far six healthy kids, and I was there for each birth. I was able to midwife the second kids during all of the births, which—thank goodness!—required only a quick toweling off and providing the mamas with some much-needed water with molasses to help them regain their strength quickly. Overall, no drama. In fact, no problems whatsoever.

But we were still waiting for Bella.

She didn't appear to be in distress, and the way she ambled around convinced me there was still a healthy baby moving around in there. So we waited.

We waited for the expected three days after Gaby gave birth, and another day and another. Our pattern of every three days was now broken. Bella started to look uncomfortable. I spent the better part of the day in the stall, sitting by her, rubbing her, and watching her. By late evening she was breathing hard. There was movement in her belly, but she wasn't standing, wasn't leaning her head against the wall, and wasn't creating a nest in the hay to prepare herself for a birth. She was clearly having trouble.

So I called the vet.

We had a wonderful barn vet, Rachel, who lived about two miles down the road and was always available if we needed her. At about nine-thirty that evening, I explained that this labor was different from the other three. I knew something was wrong. She made several suggestions for me to follow (including reaching my hand into Bella to feel around for hooves/head/butt) to determine if any of those appendages were in the wrong place, and even though I felt the hooves and head, I wasn't able to get very far in there to know if anything was wrong. She suggested waiting until midnight, and if Bella didn't push a kid out by then, to call her and she'd come.

I called her again at midnight.

Rachel came right away. Matthew was there now too, along with one of my cousins who was living on-site at the time. I was on the stall floor with Bella's head in my lap. She had been pushing, but nothing was happening. Rachel did a quick exam and determined that the kid was unable to progress down the birth canal, so she would need to do an immediate C-section if Bella and the baby were going to survive. She looked at me and said, "Are you OK with this? Because you need to decide now, or we could lose them both." Without any hesitation (or any idea of what to expect), I said, "Yes."

Rachel started to prepare Bella—and me. She said she would perform the C-section right there on the floor in the stall, with Bella resting her head on my lap. I would need to hold her head and shoulders, but hopefully, the pain medicine Rachel gave Bella would kick in quickly.

And so she began.

Within minutes she had Bella opened up, organs moved out of the way, and was reaching in to pull out a perfect white, brown, and black exact duplicate of William. She handed him to Matthew, who was ready with a towel, which he used to dry him off and elicit that magnificent *baaaaah*. Then Rachel set about expertly getting everything back into Bella and stitching her up.

The whole process took ten minutes.

We slowly moved Bella into an isolation pen on a bed of fresh hay, putting her boy beside her to get some bonding and milk, but she was so weak and tired that she closed her eyes and turned her head from him. We needed to get some milk and colostrum into him, so I squeezed some colostrum from Bella's teats while she was sleeping, and milk from one of the other mamas, to bottle-feed our little C-section baby. Then I snuggled him in next to Bella for the night.

For the next several days, as Bella healed and regained her strength, we bottle-fed her boy, whom we named Howie, and kept trying to get her to at least acknowledge him. She wasn't having anything to do with him, but Howie wouldn't give up, so neither did we.

And then it happened. On the fourth day, I walked into the stall and Bella stood up, nudged Howie, began making soft noises at him, and then moved him to her teats to begin milking. I started to cry. They did it. We did it. I did it.

I had midwifed six healthy kids. I'd had a goat C-section performed on my lap, in the middle of the night, on the floor of our stall—and both mama and baby survived. I bottle-fed Howie until Bella was ready to raise him, and in the meantime, nursed her back to health. I figured if anything qualified me as a real ranch girl, all of that did.

I had stepped into my Nxt.

Playing a Role

It's perfectly natural to feel awkward and unsure and a bit like an imposter when you enter into a Nxt phase of your life. Especially if it's super different from anything you've done before. But even if you're making a small adjustment to your career, your relationship, or your lifestyle, you can still feel like you are *faking it* or playing a role until something happens that convinces you that you belong where you are.

It's the nature of change.

I had no idea that the experience I'd need to fully step into my Nxt was to birth some goats—or have a C-section performed on my lap! That would have been a long-shot prediction at best when we chose this new lifestyle. But wouldn't it have been unreasonable to expect that I'd know what it would take to become a rancher (for myself) when we started this new life? I didn't know what I didn't know.

It could have been something else. Like learning to drive the tractor. Or bringing the cows in from the pasture. Or training the mini horses to come in from the pasture when I call them (which is special and cute, by the way). All of those things could have *qualified* me to be a rancher, if I chose to define myself as a ranch girl by those things. But I didn't. It was birthing baby goats.

When creating a Nxt for yourself, you can have a general idea of what to expect. You can identify what's important to you and define the parameters and criteria for your Nxt. But ultimately, you will need to define for yourself what it means for you to step into that Nxt. It's your call. Not your boss's. Not your partner's. *Yours.*

And typically, until you begin to live it, you don't know what you don't know. It takes experiencing your Nxt for a while to move from playing the role of your Nxt to stepping into your Nxt.

Identifying With Your Nxt Self

After I married Brian, I remember the first time someone called me by my married name.

"Mrs. Carrillo?" someone said to me.

Who? I thought.

I assumed they were addressing Brian's mother.

I had no identification with that name at that time. I barely identified with the idea of being married, let alone of being someone's wife. But as soon as we were married, I was expected to step into that new identity. It was a huge life change—my Nxt, at the time, and one that I was absolutely thrilled to enter. Still, it felt almost like an out-of-body experience: single Cindy looking across at married Cindy, not quite identifying with either, yet feeling like I had to let go of my previous self to step into my Nxt self.

It took some time before I was able to integrate the idea of being a wife into my Nxt self.

It was the same thing when I moved onto the Ranch. For a while, I identified myself in terms of my previous life—living as an imposter in my current life. I was a CEO living on a ranch. Or I was a nice suburban Jewish girl living on a ranch. So even though I was living in this Nxt phase, living this drastically new lifestyle—so different from my life before, I continued to identify as my previous self. It took a while—and birthing baby goats—for me to identify as a rancher living on a ranch. But I was still a CEO and a nice Jewish girl—living on a ranch. I had added "rancher" to my identity, but I didn't lose the other parts of me when doing so.

In working with my coaching clients, I have found that many share a fear of having to choose between their current identity and their Nxt identity—that somehow they have to *give up* the former to get to the latter. Understandably, they don't want to give up who they were to become someone new.

You don't have to give up anything. You get to add. You don't have to choose between one identity and a Nxt one. Your Nxt self will always encompass all of the parts of you—your experience, your knowledge, and your achievements (and your past titles)—when you allow those things to blend into your expanded identity. If you've worked at a large corporation with a big job, a big title, and a big salary, you don't lose that identity in your Nxt self. You build that into your Nxt identity. You are always the person who did those things—no matter what you choose to do, how you choose to work, or how much you choose to earn.

> *Your Nxt self will always encompass all of the parts of you—your experience, your knowledge, and your achievements (and your past titles)—when you allow those things to blend into your expanded identity.*

When I was no longer married to Brian, I had to rediscover my identity as a single woman. As I entered that Nxt phase of my life, I realized it *included* all of the experiences, memories, and lessons learned from that relationship. I knew that having been married to Brian was still a part of my identity and my life and always would be. Even though my Nxt self no longer identified with being married, *having been married* would always be a part of my identity.

Stepping into your Nxt requires moving from "I am this . . ." to "and now I am also this . . ." It is not an either/or. It is more. I will always be a nice suburban Jewish girl, but now I have a healthy dose of ranch girl mixed in. I will always define myself as *having been* a CEO, but now I identify that as a part of my expanded identity—as a ranch business owner. I am not married now, but that experience has made me a better partner to Matthew, and I cherish my marriage *as a part of* the identity of my Nxt self.

You don't lose who you were when you choose to step into your Nxt. You evolve. You build upon your previous self. You stand on the foundation of your different experiences, and you apply whatever you can to your Nxt self. You become more.

Important Takeaways

- ✧   It can feel really awkward and fake when you first step into your Nxt.

- ✧   You need to live your Nxt for a while before you can fully step into it.

- ✧   For a while, you will identify more with your previous life than with your Nxt life. Kind of straddling both worlds.

- ✧   Sometimes there is a fear of having to relinquish one identity before you can step into the identity of your Nxt self. But it's not an either/or. It's more.

- ✧   Stepping into your Nxt requires moving from an identity of "I have always been this . . ." to "and now I am also this . . ."

- ✧   You get to bring your whole life with you. Add it all in for an expanded brand of your identity.

- ✧   Birthing goats is an amazing experience. Even when things take a scary turn, and you end up having a C-section performed on one of your goats, on your lap, in the middle of the night, on the floor of the stall in your barn.

- ✧   Baby goats are ridiculously cute.

14

Know Your Number

CHAPTER 14

Know Your Number

Don't set your goals by what
other people deem important.

—JAACHYNMA N.E. AGU
The Prince and the Pauper

The first few years of living on the Ranch were all about building the infrastructure, which, quite frankly, meant a lot more money was going *out* the door than was coming back in. We had finished the Main House and the Guest House, expanded our guest accommodations to include a yurt and a tepee, poured a large RV pad with a full hookup, installed what seemed like miles of permanent fencing, and established all of the landscaping around the houses. We built out, planted, and fenced in a huge garden with twenty raised beds, then built a separate garage we dubbed "the Shack," because that's where Matthew put all of the equipment and stuff for the Ranch (and it's usually in a state of disarray). We added a playground (as soon as Ally told me she was pregnant with my first grandchild) and created our own little road system around what we now call "the Compound," comprising the six acres we considered to be our *living area* (as opposed to the remaining acreage we deemed to be "nature," which would be used for growing hay and as an animal habitat).

It was a lot.

Because I referred to myself as "retired" at this point, you'd think I would finally want to put on that big ol' hat and sit in that rocking chair I always talked about, to sit back and enjoy all we had achieved. Four things kept me from doing that:

1. I *liked* working. I also liked to earn, and I wasn't ready to stop doing either.

2. We needed to figure out how to financially sustain this place into the future. We had to think of ways to earn a living *from* the Ranch in order to stay living *on* the Ranch for what I believed would be the rest of our lives.

3. I really liked *business*, especially running a business, and I liked the structure a business brought to my life. I liked the systems and organization inherent within a business, so I wanted to stay engaged in running a business of some kind.

4. If done well (and if there is a market for what your business is offering), your business can become a vehicle for earning. So turning the Ranch into a business was my best strategy for earning.

The challenge was to create the right kind of business at the Ranch to fit into our lifestyle. We knew we didn't have enough acreage to earn a living entirely through ranching or farming, and honestly, I wasn't striving to become a *real* farmer or rancher. We were hobbyists. A hobbyist fits the care of their animals and the tending of their land *into* their life. A real farmer or rancher *makes it their living.*

As luck (or the Universe) would have it, as I was beginning to get itchy about earning again, our local paper published an article on the shortage of hotel rooms in the area. Hospitality had never been on my radar as a business opportunity, but I thought, *What if we turned our guest accommodations into short-term rentals?* Airbnb and VRBO had become increasingly commonplace around the world, and our area of Colorado was a very popular destination, with its huge variety of outdoor activities available year-round. There weren't a lot of Airbnbs in the area, and we already had a furnished yurt, a tepee, and a beautifully appointed Guest House we could rent out. All we'd need to do was adapt them to accommodate paying guests. Instinctively we knew hosting strangers would be different than friends and family, but it didn't concern either of us, and, seriously, what a great way to capitalize on what we already had!

Ironically, Matthew and I had never rented an Airbnb or VRBO before. We had always been *hotel* kind of people (more accurately, *I* had always been a room-service kind of person), but we figured,

> *The challenge was to create the right kind of business at the Ranch to fit into our lifestyle.*

How hard can it be? You list your property, greet people when they arrive, and clean up after they leave. Seemed straightforward. So we decided to become an Airbnb property. As with all things on the Ranch, we made up how to do it.

When I say we *made it up*, I mean we designed our rental business from the perspective of how we would like to stay at the Ranch if *we were guests*, not based on how others rented out their properties. The description of the listings, the communication with guests, the setup of the accommodations, and the check-in/check-out policies were handled in a way that *we* would have appreciated. We then added special touches: tours around the property, tractor rides for little kids, and other personal features that we believed would make our guests feel special with the *experience* of staying at CC Blue.

> *How hard can it be? You list your property, greet people when they arrive, and clean up after they leave.*

What we didn't do—*and I should have known better*—was to establish this venture with a number in our heads about what we needed (and wanted) the financial contribution of the rentals to be. We went at it with a "let's see what happens" attitude, rather than having an expectation of what we needed to earn in the short term and what we were working toward earning in the longer term. (SPOILER ALERT: This is *not* the right way to start a business.)

Honestly, we just got caught up in the energy and excitement of the idea and allowed it to move us along without consciously planning and setting expectations for the business. We started with momentum, which got us going, but we neglected to design the business with intention, which is not uncommon when starting a new business. But because we were trying to earn a living from this business, we should have started with an expectation of *how much* we needed to earn. Otherwise, how could we plan? Or budget? Or prioritize our decisions?

Simple answer? *We couldn't.* We flew by the seat of our pants and ended up being *grateful* for *any* money we brought in. (Another common trait of a new business.)

Within days of listing our rentals on Airbnb, we started getting bookings. With three levels of accommodations, we attracted three levels of guests:

1. Campers looking for a rustic *yet novel* experience would choose to sleep on the cots we provided in the bare-bones accommodation of the tepee.

2. Those who were looking for an *elevated* rustic experience would choose the yurt, which didn't have any electricity or running water, but did have a glorious four-poster bed, a beautiful sitting room area, and a wood-burning stove (a true glamping experience).

3. For guests wanting a modern and luxurious experience, our Guest House totally fit the bill.

We were thrilled that people were attracted to our property and equally thrilled that they were willing to pay to stay. As the frequency of bookings steadily increased, we spent our time managing the rentals. We spent our days on all of the communication before, during, and after the bookings, greeting our guests as they arrived (sometimes all guests arrived simultaneously), giving tours to our guests during their stay, and let's not forget about the hours we spent cleaning each place (sometimes three a day).

We were more than willing to do it all, but we soon wondered if we were making *enough* to justify all the time and effort it took to run the business. The problem: We had no idea what *enough* meant. What did we *need* to run the Ranch and the rentals? How much did we *want* to earn? How much *time* did we want to spend doing this work? And honestly, what was the big-picture goal behind running short-term rentals on the Ranch? Clearly, we didn't have enough information to answer those questions. We didn't know what the Ranch cost us, nor what it needed to earn for us.

We needed our numbers.

Do the Math

I was never very good at math. My dad was, but my mom wasn't, and I figured I was more like her than him. I rejected the idea of being good with numbers, declaring, "I'm not good at math" when I was in the third grade, although I enjoyed doing the addition tables. I did not, however, enjoy subtraction. The idea of *taking something away* was far less attractive to me (even in the third grade) than the thought of *adding more.*

> *Profitability is not a new concept, but it's an idea that has been assigned almost entirely to running a business, not to our personal lives.*

When I was a CEO and we'd have a meeting about setting annual financial targets, I'd always reiterate my base philosophy for the business. "I like big numbers, and I like adding to them," I'd say. "So no subtracting this year—just adding." It was a ridiculous statement to make and typically made everyone laugh, but it also put everyone into a mindset of growth. There was an expectation that we would grow our sales, our service offerings, our people, our infrastructure, and ultimately, our bottom line. I made it clear that we weren't in business to lose money or to become *less than* we were. We needed to grow—*to add.*

I employed the same philosophy when turning the Ranch into a business. Obviously, CC Blue Enterprises was way different from anything I'd done before, but at the same time, we were designing this business to underwrite the lifestyle we wanted to live on the Ranch. It wasn't going to be a typical company, but I still wanted to enlist my way of thinking about adding rather than subtracting as we began to monetize the Ranch and apply that simple philosophy to everything we did.

To begin, we needed to add up all of the costs associated with our life on the Ranch: living expenses, ranch expenses, and rental expenses. And because our work and lifestyle were totally intermingled, we needed to get to a number representing our total expenses.

When we completed this exercise, I became enlightened to our life on the Ranch in a completely new way. I *thought I knew* what our costs were—*kind of.* I'd been making decisions with a rough idea of the amount of money we had coming in, and a rough idea about the amount of money going out. As it turned out, I didn't have any real numbers—only assumptions. That was a problem. I was operating the finances of the Ranch (and consequently our lives) as a kind of guessing game—with more hope and belief than data.

I could hear the rationalizations in my head when we needed to make a big purchase: "I *hope* we'll have enough this month to pay for all of the animal supplies we need to stock up on." "I *believe* we have enough to pay for those repairs in the Guest House, because the last guests broke the bathroom faucet."

Who runs a business, or a life, that way?

Answer: *most of us.*

But shouldn't we all know our numbers?

Answer: *yes.*

To know your numbers, you must be willing to gather all of the information and do the math. For us, it was life-changing. Once we knew our costs, we were able to understand our *Break-even Number.* The real number that represented our current reality. The number that told us what we were spending to financially sustain our life.

Identifying your Break-even Number shows you what you *need* to earn to meet your expenses. It's your bottom line. It defines the amount of income you need to earn to maintain the life you have created. It's a crucial number for you to know!

For us, our Break-even Number was enough to sustain our current lifestyle, but *not* nearly enough for us to grow into the future lifestyle we both wanted.

What Are You Working Toward?

Once you know your Break-even Number, you can begin to take a broader view of how you want to live the Nxt stage of your life and what additional resources (money, time, etc.) you need to do so. What would you want to include in your life that you don't have now? What would you do differently? Maybe you'd go on a trip to Italy or purchase a better car. Or maybe you'd be able to take that raft trip through the Grand Canyon. It doesn't matter what it is. What matters is that you allow yourself to dream about what you want to add into your life in order to grow into your ideal Nxt. Then you can plan to get there.[*]

I can't tell you how many times my clients have said to me, "I'd love to take that trip or buy a new car, but I know I can't afford it." But when I ask, "How much additional money are we talking about?" they invariably respond, "Oh, I don't know, but I'm sure it's more than I can afford."

---

[*] Side note: As I write this, I can almost see a collective eye roll as you're all thinking, *I'd love to do that, but why would I start dreaming about what I want to add into my life if I know I can't afford it?* (That's another blocker!)

Why? Why assume you can't afford it? You might not have enough money to cover all of the costs right now, but if it's important to you and you know what you are working toward, I bet you can make a plan to get the money to pay for it. Without knowing the costs, however, you can't plan. Then I would agree; you absolutely will never be able to afford it.

Once Matthew and I knew our Break-even Number, we understood what we needed to cover the costs of the Ranch, and we could see that we were meeting that number. Great. We weren't losing money. But we wanted to expand our lifestyle and continue to develop the Ranch. So we needed to ask ourselves what we were working toward—both for the growth of the Ranch and for ourselves.

Were there things we wanted to add? More equipment we wanted to get? More ways to invest in the property to make it run more efficiently? Were there things we wanted to do in our personal lives that we weren't already doing? Travel more? Entertain more? Have more time to explore the area?

We made a list of the additional things and experiences we wanted to include in our lives, beyond what our Break-even Number would cover. It included things like international travel, a bigger tractor for the Ranch, a barn for storing our hay, and more experiential trips with our family. (Can you say, "The Wizarding World of Harry Potter"?)

We also began to think about hiring some help to free up some of our time and reduce the pain to our ever-aging bodies. We researched and estimated the cost of each item and added them up to get the total amount we'd need to accomplish them.

That became our Profit Number. Our Profit Number was the

income we needed to generate above and beyond our Break-even Number. It wasn't about sustaining our lifestyle; it was about being able to make specific choices to add to our lifestyle.

Profitability is not a new concept, but it's an idea that has been assigned almost entirely to running a business, not to our personal lives. Successful business owners don't operate with a break-even mentality. They operate with a profit mentality. They strategize and plan to earn a profit. This, in turn, allows them to grow and invest in their company and their people. When you have a personal profit mentality, you operate your life expecting you will invest in and add to your lifestyle. You make decisions based on earning more than your Break-even Number. That's how you add to your life. We should all operate our lives with a profit mentality.

Make It a Game

Many of my coaching clients have stayed stagnant in their lives, believing they can't make a change because they feel locked in *financially*. They believe they can't change their job because they earn a certain salary and don't think they can earn that same amount elsewhere. Or they can't make a needed change in their relationship because of fear: "How will we each be able to afford to live?" Or they want to stop working and retire but have no idea how much money it will take. (Retiring is loaded with all kinds of financial uncertainty.)

I get it. Money is a big issue when it comes to finding your Nxt.

So we have to deal with it. Otherwise the process of finding your Nxt is all theoretical, and you won't be able to turn your ideas into an actionable plan. If you've come this far in the process, it's time to get practical and tactical. Dealing with the money part of your Nxt is essential to moving forward.

That doesn't mean it has to be dry and mathematical and, dare I say, all about creating a budget. *Ugh.* If you want to turn someone off within ten seconds, use the word *budget.* It's like using a four-letter word, on steroids. *Nobody* wants to budget. It feels restrictive and cumbersome and boring. It does for me too.

Why not embrace your Numbers and use them to motivate yourself to move forward in the direction you intentionally set?

So I made the Break-even/Profit Number exercise into a game.

I do that with a lot of things I'd rather not deal with. It's more fun and much more engaging to make it a game. For instance, I'll set a goal for when I'll hit my Break-even Number for the year, and then set another to get to my Profit Number. This lets me create more "wins" along the way. How early in the year can I hit my Break-even Number? Hit it by June? *Win!* What do I have to do to reach my Profit Number? Cut one expense and add two more coaching clients by August? *Win!* When I get to make choices along the way, I feel more empowered and far less restricted on what I can accomplish. Making it a game adds excitement and competition—and *fun.*

For my game, I create a twelve-month spreadsheet (my game board) at the start of every year. It includes all the expense categories down the left column and all twelve months of the year across the top, with a "total" column at the end. I use historical numbers to fill in most of the spreadsheet for expenses to give me my Break-even Number, adjusting for any known changes from the previous year.

On a lower section of the spreadsheet (or you can create another game board), I list my income sources, again, filling in the columns across all twelve months with any known numbers. When I look at the total at the right, I note how close to my Break-even Number I am at the start of the year. Hopefully, I'm ahead of that number so I know I can *more than* meet my expenses and get a head start on building up my Profit Number.

Next, I create a line at the bottom of the spreadsheet for my Profit Number, which is the total of all those things we talked about adding into the "operation" of our lives for the year. Again, this number is above and beyond my Break-even Number, which is focused on meeting my known expenses. As part of my game, I like to spread my Profit Number evenly across the twelve months, because I like to try to earn a share of my annual Profit Number every month. I find it's more fun for me to take the "win" every month when I hit my number.

I track those numbers every month. It may sound time-consuming, but it allows me to play my game much more efficiently—and in real time. It also totally changes my perspective on whether or not I can afford something when we talk about adding something into our life. Instead of asking *whether* I can afford to take a trip to Italy, I "game it out" to see how I can make it happen. I plug the costs for the trip into my spreadsheet and see how it all affects my Number, so that I can shift payments around to make it work. I see how it would work if I made our airline reservations early in the year and spread out the payments on our credit card over six months, allowing us to meet our monthly

Number. Then I'll plug in the cost for our accommodations into a later month. Train tickets for in-country travel? Another month.

I *assume* we're going to Italy, plug in the numbers, and see what's needed to make it possible. Maybe we'll delay a purchase for a month. Maybe we open up more dates for Airbnb rentals another month. Instead of assuming we can't go to Italy, I *assume we will go* and use the Break-even/Profit Number game to figure out how to make it happen—and I do it in a way that works with my Numbers. I no longer limit my vision to what we have, and I never assume we can't afford to do something. Instead, I game out how and determine when we'll be able to do it.

Finding your Nxt is all about gaming out what you want your life to be. You must consider the money it will take to achieve your ideal life and make the changes you'll need to get there. But here's the thing: Without a Number, you declare that you want (and deserve) to never run your life or your business in a way that will attain that Number. You will always earn just what you need to get by and live within the confines of your Break-even Number. You will never find your Nxt.

Why not embrace your Numbers and use them to motivate yourself to move forward in the direction you intentionally set? Don't be afraid to set a higher bar for yourself. If you've already been brave enough to dream and identify what's most important to you, set the criteria for how to achieve your dream. Plan how you'll move ahead. Striving to meet a Profit Number will feel like a natural progression toward stepping into your Nxt.

Important Takeaways

- It's important to have a number based on what you *need* to live on, and a number you are working toward for the way you *want* to live.

- Employ a philosophy of adding to, not subtracting from, your life. I'm not talking about things. I'm talking about ways you can continue to grow the life you want to live.

- Do the math to determine your Break-even Number. Your Break-even Number includes all of the costs for living the life you *currently* live.

- Do the math to determine your Profit Number. Your Profit Number is the total cost to accomplish those things you identified above.

- Businesses operate with a profit mentality. To get to your Nxt, operate your life with a profit mentality.

- Make the process of working toward your Numbers a game. Set mini goals for yourself throughout the year to keep the process engaging and fun.

- Remove the word *budget* from your vocabulary. Insert the words "Break-even/Profit Number game."

- Don't be afraid to set a higher bar for yourself.

- If you haven't already gone to Italy, figure out how to get there. It's wonderful.

15

Put It on the Calendar

CHAPTER 15

Put It on the Calendar

*If you don't make the time to work on creating
the life you want, you're eventually going
to be forced to spend a LOT of time dealing
with a life you don't want.*

—KEVIN NGO
Let's Do This!

I must say that our life on the Ranch was extremely full. There was so much to do and so much to create, and it felt like we were in a constant state of motion—and list-making. I was either writing extensive lists of things to do or playing the game of adding the things *we actually did* to our list, to be able to cross things off as proof we had accomplished something each day. (I *know* I'm not the only one who does this.) I was a list-making machine, and if I do say so myself, we were becoming extremely proficient at the *crossing-off* part of the list-making process and getting some serious shit done.

Especially after we added the barn animals and the Airbnb.

Those two things, on top of everything else we had been doing, seemed to add an almost exponential amount of work to our daily routine. If I thought we were in a constant state of motion *before* we added in a barn full of animals and saw random strangers coming onto the property day in and day out, then I can only describe us as *Energizer Bunnies on steroids* during this time.

On a typical summer day, we'd begin at sunrise with barn chores; move to the garden for weeding, watering, and harvesting; and then tend to all of the other plants and flowers surrounding the houses. We'd catch a quick breakfast, and, depending on the priorities of the day, clean (any number of places), wash linens, mow lawns, irrigate the fields, fix fences, check waterers, answer rental inquires or send check-in information, brush horses, pay bills, shop for groceries and feed, fix whatever was broken on the property, prepare meals, host friends and family, and end with evening chores as the sun set over the barn.

It was a lot.

It also felt like *all* of our time was being taken up by the needs of the Ranch. The animals needed care. The rentals needed cleaning, or guests needed attention. The plants needed to be watered, and the property needed to be kept groomed and maintained. As intentional as we were about bringing animals onto the property and turning our guest accommodations into a moneymaking machine, we didn't factor in how much *time* all of it would require. I don't know who I thought would be doing the additional work (since we weren't planning on hiring any help), but somehow I missed the *time* piece of the equation when adding several more animal species—and a lot more people—to our world.

I know, I know—all of this was the result of everything *we had decided* to create and the lifestyle we had chosen. And we were loving it (I swear!), but I would be lying if I didn't admit that it was a lot of work.

On another level, however, the daily *routine* of our lives turned out to be an amazing anchor to the whirlwind of activity we were experiencing. In my pre–CC Blue life, I would have torn my hair out by the roots at the very thought of doing the same thing day in and day out. But the crazy thing about *this* routine was that it was both comforting and grounding. The repetition, the manual labor, the interaction with the land, the animals, and our guests all created their own calming effect in our daily life. Matthew thrived in that environment. He was raised in the military, so he loved the routine. It was constant and predictable and, surprisingly, it was working for both of us.

But it was also a *huge* commitment.

And the weight of that commitment got heavier the more I felt tied to the property.

For the first year after the barn animals came on-site, we didn't go anywhere overnight. We went out to dinner only occasionally because we *had* to get back to feed the animals before it got too dark. (I started to feel like my grandparents, who would go out to dinner at 5:00 because they *had* to be home by 7:00 to watch *The Ed Sullivan Show*.) It was nuts! We weren't making plans, and we weren't leaving the property.

Vacations started becoming distant memories as well. However, we *needed* to take time away. If we weren't careful (and we weren't being careful), our thirty-five acres would become a really small bubble encapsulating our lives. We loved the Ranch, but there was a big, glorious world out there, and I wanted to see as much of it as possible.

I also felt it was vital to take a break from our routine in order to get refreshed. Matthew was fine staying on the Ranch for long periods of time, running the place, doing the chores, and basically living the Ranch life, but I needed breaks away. And even though I was intentional about taking a few days off on a pretty regular basis to drive back to Boulder to spend time with Ally, A.J., and Brian and connect with friends, I felt it was equally important that *Matthew and I* spend time away from the Ranch together.

So what was going on with us? Why were we allowing ourselves to become stuck?

We weren't leaving the property because we weren't putting dates on the calendar, allowing us to *be* off-property. Without setting days off-site on our calendar, we had no way to plan for our absence. Without a plan for our absence, we couldn't leave the property. It became a vicious circle—and an excuse for staying in our routine.

Another block to leaving was the most obvious: *Who would take care of our animals?* We did everything ourselves. Being new to the community, we didn't have a network of friends and fellow ranchers to help us in an absence. And we had a problem trusting others to do things the way *we wanted things to be done*. Since we made the whole thing up, *we knew* our way wasn't the traditional way farmers or ranchers cared for their animals, so finding someone to be on-site and care for our animals the way we did was a challenge. Not an insurmountable one, but it certainly blocked us for a while.

So, as much as the animals and rentals helped us financially and created a routine that became a centering and stabilizing part of our life, we allowed it all to hold us back. It held us hostage to the life we were creating. We were allowing the priorities of the Ranch to overtake the priorities of our needs. We had to make our life more well-rounded to include more time for ourselves. We had to manage our time better, schedule differently, prioritize more intentionally, and get some help with the chores so that we felt comfortable leaving the property.

Starting with the way we managed our calendar.

In my previous lives as a mom and a CEO, I had utilized my calendar brilliantly. I was the scheduling queen. It was the only way to make sure that balls didn't get dropped, appointments didn't get missed, and activities were attended. On the Ranch, however, I let our calendar go by the wayside. I still used it as a tool for scheduling guests who would be on-site, or for my coaching calls, and I certainly put all medical appointments on it, but I wasn't using it proactively to prioritize our time.

So on a lovely summer evening, I grabbed Matthew by the arm, put a drink in his hand, and led him up to the dance hall (our place to chat about all things *Ranch* before dancing). I pulled up the calendar on my iPad and said, "Let's talk about where we want to go and when we want to go there. It's time we started putting things on the calendar that *we* want to do." He raised an eyebrow, then his glass, and we started to prioritize time for us.

Set Your Priorities

If you really want to *do* something, you have to put it on the calendar. Otherwise (as I've said before) it will not happen—at least not in the time frame you intend. Life happens. We get busy. We get distracted. It's amazing what we can do in a day, a week, or even in an hour to fill the times we haven't allocated for a specific task (especially if you're writing a book). We'll walk by the kitchen sink and wash the dishes, or clean the counters, or watch something on TV, play a video game, or simply sit and watch the paint dry—if we don't have something that *we've determined to be doing*. We can always fill our time with "doing things," just not the things we intend. The question is whether the things that fill up our hours, days, and weeks are the most important to us—or *not*. It's a choice.

> *If you really want to do something, you have to put it on the calendar.*

It would be a shame to go through the entire process of laying out your ideal dream and then fail to prioritize the things you believed were going to make your full dream come true. For example, have you defined travel as one of the most important aspects of your ideal life and set your sights on vacationing in Italy? Or dreamt about spending a few days in wine country? And it *never* happens? Years can go by, and that trip to Florence gets further and further from your sights. You begin to think it's a pipe dream. And yet, you fill your time. You do stuff. You go to work. You see friends. You travel to see family or take that camping trip. But Italy? It's too big. Too far away. Too expensive.

Of course, you're busy. You're just not doing the *right* things to reach your dream, because you don't make it a priority. Even though it's important to you.

If you really want to go to Italy or spend a few days in wine country, then you have to put it on the calendar to prioritize the time and space in your life. Otherwise, it will never happen. I swear. Activities don't become real until they have a date or a time carved out in your life to make them happen. You won't take your priorities seriously until they occupy a place on your calendar. And you can't take the necessary steps to make time to take that trip to Italy unless you identify a specific time frame in your day, your week, your month, or your year to actually do it.

If you don't set your priorities and align your calendar to them, you can't manage your life well. Matthew and I let our life get away from us because we didn't prioritize how we were allocating our time. We didn't identify the activities that were the *most important* to us and block off the space on our calendar *to do them*. Instead, the things that filled our calendar were all the things *we hadn't prioritized*. And those things were running our life.

Now, there are a lot of things in life that fill up our calendars, things we must do to meet our life's responsibilities. Meetings at work, doctors' appointments, times to drop your kids off at school and pick them up, or even hairdresser appointments. But if we don't block off time—*in advance*—for the things that we feel are most important, all the other things will dominate our time (always), and the things we want to prioritize will never happen. We let routine trump intention. We let the urgent smother the important. Why? Because trips to Italy or wine country don't typically happen *in the moment.* They happen when we intentionally set time aside on our calendars to allow them to happen—and then work toward making them a reality.

The most obvious mistake we made was failing to schedule time on our calendar for when *we didn't want* guests on the property. Theoretically, we controlled the Airbnb calendar, and yet we kept the whole damn year open for guests—and ultimately felt tied to the property. *We* did that. Nobody forced us to open our space to guests year-round. We could have strategically scheduled ways to prioritize our time both on and off the Ranch. It wasn't difficult; we just needed to commit to it.

Remarkably, once we decided to prioritize how we wanted to spend our time, and put those things on the calendar, we no longer felt trapped in the life we had created.

We started to live the life we *really* wanted to live.

Make a Commitment

Until you put it on the calendar, it's all just talk.

Here's the real scoop: Until you identify a date that you're going to take that trip to Bali you've been talking about since reading *Eat, Pray, Love* in your twenties, or quit that job you've been miserable doing since your boss left and that crazy lady started supervising you, or marry that person you've been head-over-heels in love with for the past six years—*it ain't gonna happen.* Days turn into weeks. Weeks turn into months, and, unfortunately, months turn into years and years and years. You keep talking about it, but you never *do it.*

Because you haven't made *a commitment* to *do it.*

It's easy to talk about going on a trip or quitting your job or someday marrying your true love, but until you prioritize it by setting aside the time to do it, it doesn't really have *you* behind it. You're not invested. Other things will fill up your time. Other activities will fill the void. Other priorities will push it aside.

Putting it on the calendar is the act of committing to do something. It's *you* deciding what *you* are going *to do*.

It doesn't have to be a big thing like taking a trip to Bali, quitting your job, or getting married. It can be getting your hair cut (which, by the way, can be a big deal), or going camping for the weekend at the lake half an hour away, or inviting your favorite friends for a pizza/ game night in two weeks. If you want to *do* things, then you need to make the time to do them. You need to set a day and a time for that activity. And it begins with the commitment to do it.

> *Putting it on the calendar is the act of committing to do something. It's you deciding what you are going to do.*

Often, we schedule our time automatically—like setting an appointment to get our hair cut—so we don't attribute a lot of commitment to making that happen. But the same practices and mindset for setting aside our time, figuring out the logistics, and having enough money to cut the hairs on our head also need to be employed for the big stuff we want to do.

For example, once you make the commitment to go to Bali (woo-hoo!) and you have the dates blocked off on your calendar, you now have a framework (and a time frame) to start making plans. You can figure out the logistics of getting there and back, decide where you're going to stay, set aside the money, arrange for time off from work, and, most importantly, figure out what you're going to pack—all because your intention of going to Bali has been made a priority. You made the commitment to do it, and you put it on your calendar to make it happen. Your plan is set—you just need to follow it through.

Once Matthew and I made the commitment to travel and prioritized time on our calendar to get off the property, we were able to move through the block of finding someone to take care of our animals when we were gone. For the first couple of years, we just assumed we couldn't find anyone to do all of the chores the way we did. I don't know why; it isn't rocket science. But it wasn't really about the work. We just didn't have a reason to look for someone until we committed to going somewhere and knew *when* we were going. Until then, it would have been silly to have a conversation with someone about watching the Ranch for us.

"Hey, would you like to come and stay at the Ranch to take care of our animals when we're gone?"

"Sure. When?"

"I don't know. We haven't made the commitment to go anywhere yet."

Silence.

Until we put it on the calendar, it would have just been talk, without any context.

Finding your Nxt is about figuring out *which dream you want to pursue, why* you want to do it, and *how* best to accomplish it. Once you know those things, *then* you must commit to doing it and set a time frame for *when* it will happen. It's the only way to move from *finding* your Nxt to *doing* your Nxt.

Now Do It

Once you put your Nxt on the calendar and make the commitment to do it, you've progressed from dreaming about it to seeing it laid out in front of you, to defining what's important to you, to intentionally deciding how best to move forward, to setting a time frame to take *action* and make it happen.

Now you can actually do it.

Sometimes it feels risky and scary when you set a time frame to finally *do your Nxt*. All the blockers can start raising their evil little heads again when you're getting ready to launch your Nxt, because you don't know everything that can happen and you don't know whether you'll be successful. But declaring when you will begin your Nxt allows you to work backward within the assigned time frame and create a plan. It provides a timeline to set benchmarks and deadlines to guide you. And it moves your thinking beyond the theoretical, giving you context to work within. All of this reduces the unknown and the prospect of failure, because you're moving forward with an intentional action plan.

Dream trips, dream jobs, and dream houses don't become a reality unless you move your *intention* into a *commitment*. When you layer a time frame on top of it—you'll have a framework for actually doing your Nxt.

For Matthew and me, we knew that if we didn't block off our calendar for our own time (on or off the property—it didn't matter), it would never happen. Our life was full, and we would always fill it up with a hundred different things—just not the things we wanted to prioritize. When we put time *for ourselves* on the calendar, we were able to restructure the way we were living, and it felt good to prioritize what was important to us again.

It made me realize that we could always reimagine how we were setting up this lifestyle for ourselves, allowing it to evolve as our needs and wants changed. It felt like we were making it up again. Stepping into another level of our Nxt. Readjusting our priorities for the way we spent our time based on how we wanted to work and live on the Ranch moving forward.

It would be a shame to go through the entire process of laying out your ideal dream and then fail to prioritize the things you believed were going to make your full dream come true.

As a result, we started *doing* all the things we wanted to do.

We were putting trips on the calendar (no longer limiting ourselves to a specific time of year) and planning for them by scheduling things so we *could* go away. We blocked dates from the Airbnb calendar so we wouldn't have guests on-site while we traveled. We planned our Ranch projects based on when we were in town. We were able to find people to care for the Ranch in our absence, had plenty of time to get on *their* calendars (which was as big a deal as getting the trip on *our* calendar), and get them trained before we left. And we could plan the logistics and details of each of our trips to ensure they were as dreamy as we hoped they would be.

What's the moral of this story? Use your calendar as a tool to prioritize what's important to you. Make a commitment to do it, and then *just do it.*

Important Takeaways

✧ Prioritize what's important to you, then allocate a block of time on your calendar to do it.

✧ Until you put it on the calendar, it's all just talk.

✧ You need to make a commitment, or your Nxt will never happen.

✧ The simple act of putting the steps of your Nxt on the calendar moves it toward action.

✧ Dream trips, dream jobs, and dream houses don't become a reality unless you move your intention to a commitment.

✧ Routine doesn't have to make you want to pull your hair out by the roots; it can be a great anchor to the whirlwind of your life.

16

---

*Create the
Perfect Blend*

CHAPTER 16

Create the Perfect Blend

*Coaching is unlocking a person's potential
to maximize their own performance.*

—SIR JOHN WHITMORE
Coaching for Performance

Ffrom the start of finding this Nxt chapter of my life, I sought
to create the perfect blend of my lifestyle, my relationship,
and my work to create my ideal life. I was so fortunate to have
had all the life experiences leading up to this time, and all the
resources that my exit from the business afforded me, but it was
on me to combine all of the ingredients to live this Nxt dream. The
property—CC Blue—was obviously the lifestyle piece that provided
the foundation for everything else. My relationship with Matthew
made it all possible, because I certainly couldn't, and definitely
wouldn't, want to do any of this without him. But there's one last

important part of the mix that I haven't talked much about, and that would be my work as a coach.

This whole book represents my perspective as a coach. All of the lessons, philosophies, and teachings sprinkled throughout these pages have come from my years in business, my years as a mentor, and my experiences as a business coach. So I thought it was time to complete my story by giving you a little background about my work as a coach, which has become one of the key ingredients in forming who I've become at this stage of my life. For me, coaching taps everything I've ever been and everything I've become. It's a huge part of creating the perfect blend of my life on the Ranch.

I think I was born to be a coach. Definitely not the sports kind of coach, because athleticism was never a big part of my makeup, but, rather, a life and business coach.

I've always been that go-to person for my family, friends, and co-workers whenever they've needed to work through a problem or grab an opportunity. I've always been able to listen intently, ascertain (pretty darn quickly) what underlying issue(s) might be getting in the way, and lead a conversation about ways to move forward.

In my late 20s, I decided to get a master's degree in social work (MSW), not knowing exactly how I'd use that training and degree, but somehow I could see that it would come in handy, both in the short term and later on. Truth be told, the other (main) reason I chose that degree was that it didn't require a written thesis (God knows I never wanted to write something as long as a book—*head slap!*), but hindsight says it was an astute choice nonetheless.

One thing's for sure: I definitely didn't think I'd use my MSW to start a business, but man, did it turn out to provide me a solid foundation for running a company. Training in the art and science of social work gave me a gold mine of insights, behavioral strategies, and tools to use daily as the leader of my company. And yet, I always had a glob of insecurity sitting deep in the pit of my stomach because I didn't have an MBA as a credential for running a company. It was hard enough being a young woman starting a business with oodles of imposter syndrome plaguing me for the first few years, and not having a business degree to validate me kept the question of "Am I worthy?" front and center for a good chunk of the time while leading my company.

Luckily, over time (probably too much time), I realized that the business stuff of profit-and-loss statements, sales strategies, and operational systems were skills I could learn on the job or hire amazing people to do. The people side of the business, however, was clearly a part of my DNA, and all of the important leadership skills necessary for becoming an effective CEO benefited wildly from the social-work side of my training and my brain.

After I sold my company and began to imagine the Nxt stage of my life, I began to lean into my social-work side again and began to see myself as a coach. The timing was perfect. It takes a certain amount of life being lived and business being experienced in order to be of service and add value to someone as a coach. It requires a certain amount of "been there, done that" to be effective. In other words, it seemed like a great career move for someone like me, someone who was old enough, had accomplished something notable, and could offer a bunch of insights, lessons, and a bit of wisdom to those who were interested in being coached to accomplish their own notable thing.

Still, I had concerns.

Interestingly enough, I had a coach when I was a CEO and found the experience to be invaluable. I also joined a CEO Support Group (as I called it) with leaders of similar-sized companies who were experiencing the same kinds of growing pains within their businesses. We'd meet monthly and talk about everything from staffing issues to budget projections. Then I'd meet with my coach a couple of times a month to work on issues that were specific to me and my business.

The best thing about having a coach was having access to an outside objective human to talk with—who also had my best interest at heart. He had been in business for years, grew a company, and was willing to share a bunch of experiences and lessons learned that I could apply to my company. And honestly, it was nice to have someone to talk to, someone who had been there and done something like what I wanted to do—because running a company can be lonely.

So when I was thinking about becoming a coach, I called *my* coach. I told him what I was thinking about doing and shared my concern that I might not have everything it took to add enough value to the people I worked with.

"I don't want to fuck up anyone's life," I told him.

He chuckled.

Seriously, he actually *chuckled.*

I asked, "Why are you laughing at me?"

He said, "Cindy, you have essentially been coaching people your entire life. If you choose to do it now—*professionally*—figure out who you want to be as a coach and what your methodology will be. Then there will be no way you can fuck it up."

He added, "If this is what you are meant to do, *be intentional about it!*"

He was right. If this was what I was meant to do Nxt, I had to do it right and figure out what coaching would look like for me.

So I took myself through the process of becoming crystal clear on why I wanted to coach, before stepping into the role. And I did it exactly the same way I went through the process of finding my Nxt lifestyle on the Ranch, and the same way Matthew and I found our Nxt step in our relationship.

I had to take myself through the process of finding my Nxt way of working.

Over the course of several weeks, I figured out what was most important to me about working in this Nxt stage of my life. I decided whom I would be best suited to work with (individuals and business partners), what I would focus on to help others (growing a business and finding my Nxt), how I wanted to work (at CC Blue—on a schedule that would allow me to blend my work with my family, hosting, ranching, and time with Matthew), and why I wanted to coach (because I absolutely love working with people to help them move forward with all of their awesomeness). Once I knew all of that, I knew coaching was the next piece of the puzzle for completing the fullness of my Nxt.

From Balance to Blend

I feel like I need to apologize to everyone who has ever bought into the idea of *work/life balance*. I used to be a huge proponent through my company, which was built on the premise that the ultimate goal for anyone who worked was to balance their work and life. My company operated in the space of work/life benefits, and at the time, I was a true believer in the idea of balance. I'd go out and sell our services with the absolute conviction that our backup care benefit would help provide a balanced work and life to our clients and employees.

> *When you recognize that your work is a part of your life, you think about work as an integrated piece of your total life.*

I still believe the service we developed helped thousands of families meet some of their caregiving needs, but I wasn't selling only our service. I was selling work/life balance as an ideal of what it meant to be a parent who worked in a setting (especially for women) fraught with unrealistic expectations.

I know because I lived with those expectations. When I started my company, I was a young mother of two children, working a full-time job, and hell-bent on the idea of being able to do and have it all. I would roll up my sleeves every morning and attack the day, believing I could *be* everything to everyone and *do* everything for everyone too. I always hit the ground running. I'd get Ally and A.J. ready for school, get myself out the door for work, run the company until 3:00, rush back home to meet the school bus (often following it to our driveway), get the kids settled, and try to do a little more work, get dinner ready, put the kids to bed, and then do more work before checking in with Brian to see how his day had gone.

At the end of every day, I felt like a complete fraud—*on every level*. Not feeling like a great mom. Not feeling like a great worker or boss. And don't even get me started on my feelings about not being a good spouse. Because being a working mom is hard. Being the leader of a company is hard. Being in a relationship is hard. It was all so exhausting. And there was absolutely no balance. None. And, truthfully, there was no chance of ever achieving it.

But I'd still go out there day after day and preach the benefits of trying to create a balanced life, because our society has been obsessed with the idea of striving for work/life balance since before the first person ever hired another to do something for them. The concept, however, had several flaws, which have taken me years to reckon with, so I'm thrilled to be able to finally clear the air (and my conscience).

With that apology now issued, let's talk about work/life balance.

Let me begin with a visual.

When I think of balance, I picture Lady Justice. You know, the statue of the blindfolded lady holding a set of scales in one hand— which Lady Justice is tirelessly trying to keep balanced—and a sword in the other. (*The fact that she is also blindfolded and has a sword in one hand should not be lost on any of us, for both justice and work/life balance.*)

If we use Lady Justice to visualize the challenge of balancing *work and life*, you (being Lady Justice) get to have two pans on your bar (the little platforms where you place things to determine their weight): 1) your work pan and 2) your life pan. The work pan is filled with the everyday work you do in your job, but it can also be filled with *all* work-related stuff—like work travel, after-hours work, work deadlines causing you to work too much, and even work perks (like playing golf with the boss or going to work-related events).

Your life pan includes *everything else.*

So flaw #1 is that the concept of work/life balance has your *life pan* jam-packed with everything beyond the work-related stuff: family, friends, kids, pets, exercise, vacations, paying bills, school, extracurricular activities, grocery shopping, coffee with friends, concerts, pottery classes—*everything else.* And there's no way everything else in life can fit on one pan. It's not fair, and I'm pretty sure the physics wouldn't work. Which leads me to the second flaw.

Flaw #2 assumes your work and your life are two *separate* things. But let's be clear: Your work is not separate from your life. It may be a honkin' big *part of your life,* but it's not a separate thing. When you separate work from your life (as in, trying to balance it against the rest of your life), it's easy to think of your work as *competing* with everything else that fills that other pan, putting your work *at odds with* your life. This is a rotten (and all-too-common) way for us to view our work.

When you recognize instead that your work is *a part of* your life, however, you think about work as an integrated *piece* of your total life. Something that enhances and helps to make your whole life all it can be. No competition with the other parts of your life.

Imagine that.

Flaw #3 is the assumption that balance implies *equality.* Equality of time, effort, attention, and importance. All of the different parts of our life are not equal. And yet, the expectation behind achieving balance is to provide equal time, effort, attention, and importance to everything we have and do. Which is just insane—and quite unrealistic.

So let's stop looking at our lives as if we have two pans that are separate and distinct from one another—and let's stop making a life goal of keeping everything in balance.

Instead, let's think about all the different parts of our lives as *ingredients* that we get to *blend* to create an amazing stew—with life being the pot. Work is an ingredient, as are our family, friends, pets, vacations, extracurricular activities, coffee dates, and even our pottery classes. They are all ingredients we choose to mix together, in different configurations at different times of our lives—with the intention of creating a delicious life.

Blending the Ingredients of Life

So much of our effort in creating CC Blue was to intentionally pick all of the best ingredients of our life to create the best, most delicious Nxt chapter of our lives. We created our *Big Why* for the lifestyle we wanted to live, with all of the things we felt were most important to us, and we threw them into the life stew pot: a place for family and friends to come, a self-sustaining life, a place to dance, and an environment that was welcoming and fun. We then added animals and figured out how to do this whole ranching thing. Then we incorporated a method to earn from the Ranch through hosting short-term rentals and through various farm-produced products we sold to our guests. And, of course, I stepped into another Nxt (within my bigger Nxt) and became a coach as well as a rancher.

Once we got the hang of doing everything, I tried to imagine a way to incorporate some of the most treasured parts of our life—hosting, coaching, and experiencing the land and lifestyle of the Ranch—into a new and perfect blend for me and Matthew as we looked ahead at the Nxt evolution of life at CC Blue. (Because God knows, we weren't done making it up!)

After about ten years, some things were beginning to change. We knew we were coming to an end with the short-term rentals when we found ourselves dreading (maybe a strong word but leaning in that direction) when Airbnb guests were scheduled to arrive—and almost jubilant when we got a cancellation. I'd say that was a strong indication that we no longer wanted to have strangers coming and going. Instead, we wanted to have a lot more time open to hosting friends and family for visits. It was time to reclaim our calendar for the activities we wanted to initiate.

We also wanted to capitalize on my coaching by working with clients in person at CC Blue. I had an idea for a coaching program *at the Ranch,* which I was struggling to bring into focus. I kept thinking about ways to blend my coaching with our hosting (yes, it sort of rhymes) to create a way for clients to come to the Ranch, but my thoughts always ended up on a traditional program of hosting corporate groups for team building or strategic-planning retreats. Which was not a good fit. We had designed CC Blue with families in mind. We weren't designed for corporate groups. If corporate groups were to come, we'd have to ask the VP of Sales to share a bathroom with the VP of Operations (or even a bed), which wouldn't be a good thing (or at least not professional). So I needed to figure out other ways to bring it all together. Plus, I didn't particularly like working with groups. I've always been more of a *one-on-one kind of gal.* So the whole corporate-group idea was a nonstarter.

I could see it: the idea of working with clients here, but I couldn't visualize how it would work—until one day it hit me. What if we invited individuals (or business partners) to come to CC Blue for an immersive experience of coaching and being a part of the lifestyle we lived on the Ranch? We could host them on the property, and I could coach them about finding their Nxt—while they experienced all that we had created here at CC Blue in finding our Nxt.

It would be a partnership between me (the coach), Matthew (the supreme host and amazing cook), and CC Blue (our unique and inviting environment with beautiful views).

We'd call it *The Immersion: Finding Your Nxt.*

We would combine the perfect blend of ingredients of our lives. We would offer clients an opportunity to get out of their current reality and come to a place where all of the attention would be on them as they began their journey to figuring out their Nxt. No groups. Just them. (Two people at the most.) With a little pampering, a lot of personal attention, and the opportunity to become crystal clear on how to move forward into the Nxt stage of their lives.

Important Takeaways

- Life is not about finding work/life balance (and I apologize for my role in promoting that viewpoint earlier in my career). It's about finding the right *blend.*

- Work/life balance is flawed on several levels. For example, it sets work up as competing with the rest of your life.

- Think of all of the parts of your life as ingredients that can be blended to make a delicious life.

- Your wants and needs change over time. Your life evolves. So don't be afraid to blend different ingredients at different times of your life to best serve you at each stage.

- Each Nxt step in your life is an opportunity to do something new and exciting and opportunistic.

- Even though you might think you can't even write a thesis, one day you might end up writing a book.

Find Your Nxt—
Again and Again

F inding your Nxt is a lifelong process. You're never done—at least you shouldn't be—because every stage in your life is an opportunity to make a Nxt chapter. And each Nxt can be a transformational change that involves something new, something exciting, and something opportunistic.

I think of finding your Nxt as a "rinse and repeat" process that can be applied over and over as you move from one Nxt to another. If I've done my job effectively, you now have a blueprint of how to find your Nxt again and again.

Here are the main points to remember:

⋄   Each Nxt begins when you decide to initiate a change. Those changes can happen in the areas of your work, your relationships, and your lifestyle. Be conscious of the ripple effect each change might bring and be prepared to provide context around the change(s) you initiate.

✧ Many of us were raised believing we get only one chance to dream, so we spend our entire lives chasing one big audacious dream. However, you get to have many dreams along the way. It's not worth your time or energy to create fantasy dreams when you can create wonderful, fulfilling dreams based on your skills and strengths. So capitalize on your superpowers. Identify them, embrace them, and use them to step into all of your Nxts.

✧ The Fear of Failure (remember, we fail only if we fail to learn), the Fear of the Unknown (which is solved through the gathering of information), and the Willingness to Settle (which is destroyed through dreaming and acknowledging that you always deserve more) are always lurking around a corner, waiting to block each Nxt. Keep an eye out for them, and don't be afraid to kick them to the curb. They can't block you from moving forward if you don't let them.

✧ Don't forget to close your eyes and imagine the possibilities of the life you really want to live. Sometimes the limitations of your current reality will try to limit your vision, but trust what you see and paint a picture in your mind of the ideal life you want your Nxt to be.

✧ You are armed with the trifecta of tool kits that will always help you identify important questions, understand where you need to fill in missing information, and identify dangers lurking around the corner. Trust your gut. And know that when you find alignment within your head, heart, and gut, you can be certain you're on the right track.

✧   Keep your list of what's most important up-to-date as your life evolves. Be clear on your *Big Why* so you can use those values and criteria as a filter for your decision-making.

✧   It is vital to always move toward your Nxt intentionally. You can harness momentum to take you further down your course but make intentional decisions to move in one direction or another and, when the time is right, put a stake in the ground and declare your Nxt out loud!

✧   Remember the importance of getting to a decision to do your Nxt by putting it on the calendar, creating an action plan, and then actually stepping into your Nxt to begin living that life.

✧   Keep your eye on your numbers to make sure your Nxt is keeping you on track with your financial goals.

✧   Be diligent and intentional about how you factor all the ingredients of your life into each Nxt phase. The point isn't to try to achieve balance in your life; the trick is to find the right blend that provides you the life you really want to live.

⋄   Finally, please know you can be perfectly satisfied with what you have and still want more. Life is about growth—and learning—and everything you've done before gets to accompany you at each Nxt stage of your development.

I wish you the best in your journey, and I hope that whatever Nxt you seek, it encompasses another big audacious dream, again and again.

ACKNOWLEDGMENTS

Thank you to Tanja Pajevic, an accomplished memoir writer and teacher of writing, who listened intently when I first told her I was writing a book—and then sent me her list of the "10 steps to writing your first book"—which made me realize I had already fucked up the first four steps. (*Head slap!*)

This led her to introduce me to my incredible book coach, Rick Killian of Killian Creative. Rick listened to my idea and immediately suggested that he and his wife, Melissa, visit CC Blue Ranch to hold a mini-Immersion about the book—sealing the deal for me—and launching me into one of the most influential and meaningful learning experiences of my life. Rick guided me through the writing process, cajoled me to keep moving forward whenever I got stuck, and educated me on how to think about my reader (like an author).

A huge thank-you to my dear friend Karen Ericksen, who convinced me to let her read the first few chapters of a very early draft, then, with the utmost tenderness, cheered me on to continue writing, even though we both knew it needed a ton of work.

To Ally Carrillo, who has always been my greatest cheerleader (in every way) and who pushed me to kick some ass on this book from the first instant I started writing. To A.J. Carrillo, who read the first chapter of my shitty first draft and *still* encouraged me to write the book. And to Nicole Carrillo, and Lindsay Sutula, who each read chapters of the final draft(s) throughout the process and kept me going with their heartfelt and honest feedback, exuberance, and love.

To Brian Carrillo—who has never stopped loving me, trusting me, and believing in me no matter how much we have transformed our relationship, and for reading the manuscript with such excitement and pride that it made me want to share the book with the world.

To my brother, Brian (Buddy) Kram, who has always trusted my decisions in life and who has—since the day I was born—had my back. To my cousin/sisters Carol Glenn and Marcialee Brahms, who have always believed I could do anything I set out to do. And to Nancy Natow Cassidy—my dearest friend from the tender age of eight, who has always encouraged me to pursue every single dream I've ever had.

To Erin Weed, whose raw enthusiasm for life (and for me) pushed me forward whenever I needed a pick-me-up when writing, and whose utter faith in my ability to make shit up for each Nxt thing in my life keeps me doing just that. And to Carrie and Michael Kellman, who made me a fanatic about keeping my use of commas to their appropriate minimum and who always supported whatever I set out to do Nxt.

To my trusted friend Mike Franson, whose belief in my instinct to sell my company allowed it to happen and who personally ushered it through to its successful conclusion. And to my rock star team and colleagues at Work Options Group—who (quite literally) made running that business the most fulfilling and joyful work experience of my life.

To Amy Graham, whose undying support has always made me feel like I'm wrapped in a warm blanket. And to Thomas Vela, who swooped in at the final stages of my writing to talk through the concepts and lessons in the book, assuring me there was value in sharing them.

To my rock star Realtor, Michelle Klippert, for being such a monumental help in finding the property, and to Jeff Borchardt for seeing and designing the structures that made my dream come true. And to Katie and Jason Merkley for teaching us just about everything we know about cows, chickens, haying, and ranching.

To all the women at Top Fox Marketing—who have provided outstanding marketing and support for my coaching business, for my book, and for me, through their die-hard belief in what I do as a coach.

To my amazing copyeditor, Todd Hafer, who understood from the beginning what I wanted to achieve from this book and honored my intentions and my words (as much his editing professionalism would allow). To Peter Gloege, my talented book designer, who captured exactly what I was hoping for in the look and feel of this book. And to Elizabeth Frick and Christy Phillippe, who so diligently proofread the manuscript to make sure we didn't miss anything small or important.

And, last but certainly not least—to Matthew Valadez for always being there for me; for his willingness to drop whatever he was doing to read whatever I had just written; for dealing with every mood swing, every drop in self-confidence, and every exhilarating high. For running everything on the Ranch (always) and for stepping up as my partner to bring my Coaching Immersion program to life. And especially, for his eagerness to enter each Nxt phase of our life together with complete openness to whatever lies ahead.

Cindy Carrillo received her Master of Social Work (MSW) degree from the University of Denver and in 1986 founded Work Options Group, a leading provider of Work/Life solutions for employees of Fortune 500 companies. She built and led that company over twenty years until intuition told her it was time to sell. She put the business up for sale just days before the beginning of the financial crisis of 2008, sold it to a Fortune 100 company before the end of the year, and stayed on as its CEO into 2009.

After the sale, Cindy used her more than forty years of business experience—including private enterprise, retail, nonprofit, and government sector work—to start two new ventures: Nxt Business Coaching and CC Blue Ranch. The combination of these two led to the creation of a unique coaching experience, "The Immersion," where clients join Cindy at her ranch for a two-day deep dive into formulating a plan for the next transformational phase of their lives—what Cindy calls "Finding Your Nxt."

Cindy and her partner in transformation and life, Matthew, live on the thirty-five acres of CC Blue Ranch near Ridgway, Colorado, along with a menagerie of cattle, chickens, donkeys, geese, goats, and miniature horses, overlooking Mount Sneffels and the magnificent San Juan Mountain range. It's a lifestyle you have to experience to believe.